I CHOSE CAPITOL PUNISHMENT

By Art Buchwald

I Chose

ART BUCHWALD

Capitol Punishment

ILLUSTRATED BY *Laszlo Matulay*

CLEVELAND AND NEW YORK

THE WORLD PUBLISHING COMPANY

Published by The World Publishing Company
2231 West 110th Street, Cleveland 2, Ohio

Published simultaneously in Canada by
Nelson, Foster & Scott Ltd.

Library of Congress Catalog Card Number: 63-18589

FIRST EDITION

Contents

CONTENTS

3. ANYBODY FOR FISCAL TRAINING?

4. MANAGING THE NEWS

5. INSTANT CULTURE

6. COLD WARS, HOT LINES

CONTENTS

CONTENTS

Good-bye, Paris, Good-bye

IT IS NOT my intention to write a sad farewell to Paris, particularly since I hope to go back in two years and pick up
where I left off, which was watching several lovely girls walking down the Avenue des Champs Elysées, past Fouquet's
restaurant.

When I arrived in Paris fourteen years ago I had only one
piece of luggage. I left with thirty-four pieces of luggage. I
still had one piece of luggage; my wife's clothes accounted
for the other thirty-three.

It was hard to wrench myself away after so many years; I
don't know how many French governments I had lived
through, but from an American's standpoint nothing much
ever changed under any of them.

Even prices haven't changed since 1948. If anything they've
gone down. When I first arrived I lived in a hotel where I
paid fifty cents a night for a room. I went over to the hotel
just before I left and discovered six French-Algerian refugees
living in the same room for nothing.

All my friends in Paris seemed very happy that I was going.
To them they were not not losing a friend, but gaining an
apartment.

There is no doubt I'm going to miss certain things.

I'm going to miss breakfasting with General de Gaulle, taking long walks with Brigitte Bardot, painting Pablo Picasso's
portrait, and sitting at a sidewalk café with Greta Garbo.

I'm going to miss going dancing with Gene Kelly in Mont-
martre, and singing with Edith Piaf under one of the bridges
of the Seine. I'm going to miss water-skiing with Princess
Grace, poker games with the Rothschild family, soirees at

13

Versailles with the Duchess of Windsor, and laughs with General Raoul Salan at Santé prison.

I'm going to miss candlelight dinners with Elizabeth Taylor, and golf games with General Norstad, scrabble games with André Malraux, and parachute jumps with Ambassador Gavin.

I'm going to miss doing business with Aristotle Onassis and taking moonlight rides with Elsa Maxwell.

Not that I've done any of these things. But I'm going to miss them anyway.

Many people warned me that I was making a big mistake going to Washington, D. C. They pointed out that it's perfectly all right to make fun of the French but it's another matter making fun of Americans. Besides, they say people take themselves very seriously in Washington and there is no room for frivolity in the nation's capital at this time.

Well, I have no intention of being frivolous. No country of 180,000,000 people and a yearly deficit of nine billion dollars can afford to laugh, and I hope that if I ever write anything from Washington that is not serious and solemn, someone will throw me into the Attorney General's nearest swimming pool.

I.

ROUGHING IT
ON THE
NEW FRONTIER

Our Town

(WITH APOLOGIES TO MY GOOD FRIEND,
THORNTON WILDER)

STAGE MANAGER: The name of the town is Washington, D. C.
—just across the Maryland State line. It's a nice town, y'know
what I mean? Nobody remarkable ever come out of it s'far
as we know. We're just plain, simple folk here, and we can't
claim to be nothing more than just another town along Route
No. 1.

I better show you around a bit. That large white house over
there is the home of the Kennedy family. They rented it for
four years, with an option for another four. Not that they
couldn't afford to buy, but the owners wouldn't sell. The
Kennedys are kind of important around here, since they're
the only family in town that owns a pony. Hello there,
Macaroni!

Over there on the hill is what folks in our town call the
Capitol. Not too much been happening there recently. You
can hear a lot of yelling and screaming from the Hill, though
people are apt not to pay too much attention to it.

Well, as I said, it's just about morning and people are starting to go to work. There's Lyndon, just got back from a trip.
Hi, Lyndon. How did Ladybird like Turkey?

LYNDON: Jus' fine, jus' fine.

STAGE MANAGER: As you can see, there's nothing uppity
about the people in our town. Look, there's a light on over
there in the Pentagon. Let's wander over and see what's going
on. Hi, General. What's new?

GENERAL: Nothing much. Just moving some troops around
Asia, planting some missile sites in Alaska, and keeping tabs
on armored cars in Berlin.

STAGE MANAGER: Well, have fun, General. Things are starting to buzz over at the State Department factory about this time. There's Dean. I see you got some mail, Dean.

DEAN: Same old stuff. Notes on disarmament, South Viet-Nam, North Korea, Communist China, Argentina, Laos, Algeria, and de Gaulle. Nothing ever changes around here.

STAGE MANAGER: That's what I've been telling the folks. People 'round here have the same problems as people everywhere. Well, let's skip a few hours and go over and see one of our Senators at lunch. Senator, what's on the docket for today?

SENATOR: I have it on reliable information that the Russians sent five aircraft carriers and two Sputniks to Cuba last week. I'd like to say that I think this is the most dangerous—

STAGE MANAGER: Thanks, Senator, we have to be moving along. I see Billie Sol over by the grain elevator. Billie Sol don't live in our town, but he's a frequent visitor here. Hello, Billie, you planting any cotton this year?

BILLIE SOL: Shucks, no. Bad year for cotton planting. Think I'll just lay off for a spell and take it easy.

STAGE MANAGER: Good idea, Billie. No sense killing yourself with taxes what they are.
We got a few foreigners in our town, too. There's Serge Orlov, a Russian fellow. Lives out there in the embassy section. Hello, Serge. What are you doing today?

SERGE: Spying.

STAGE MANAGER: Serge's a real quiet fellow. Nothing uppity about him, either. Here comes our public prosecutor. Hello, Bobby. What's new down at the courthouse?

BOBBY: Nothing much. Antitrust suits, integration problems, Jimmy Hoffa, kidnapings, bank holdups, gambling cases, espionage, and my kid brother Teddy's election. Hardly enough to keep me busy. Might take a trip around the world.

STAGE MANAGER: There's one of our nine judges. Hello, Earl. Anybody want to impeach you today?

EARL: Haven't picked up my mail yet. I've been over at the public school praying with the kids.

STAGE MANAGER: Well, it's getting on to bedtime. There's a party going on over there at the French Embassy, the Shrivers are having a cookout for the Peace Corps, and the Kennedys are having Leonard Bernstein and the Philharmonic Orchestra in for a quiet evening at home. Outside of that, most people in our town are tucked in for the night after another uneventful day.

Hmm. It's eleven o'clock. Good night, all.

In Time of Crisis

LIVING IN WASHINGTON during a time of crisis can be a very nerve-racking experience. Having lived through two dozen crises in Paris during the past fourteen years, I think I'm in a good position to compare the differences between the two.

For one thing, in Paris you rarely meet the people involved in a crisis. Occasionally you run into a French spokesman at a bistro, but for the most part the people working on a French crisis are complete strangers and unavailable to the foreign press. Therefore, since the crisis is being handled by people you don't know, you have the feeling the situation is well in hand, and if all else fails, General de Gaulle will save the day.

But in Washington it's entirely different. Your next-door neighbor may be the person involved with the crisis, and you not only know him, but you know his kids.

The guy who is out there on Sunday painting his fence, or raking his leaves, is the same guy who is in charge of working out the master plan for the Joint Chiefs of Staff. The fellows you play poker with are in charge of decisions that could affect everybody. And it doesn't make you feel any better if you bluff one of them out of a hand.

In Washington your dinner partner could be the wife of an important official, and it scares you to wonder how much influence she has on her husband's decisions. And it isn't beyond belief that a congressman or Senator in charge of world-shaking events could pinch your wife under the table. While this is human, it also scares the devil out of you.

In Paris there are no secrets when it comes to a crisis. As a matter of fact, there are so many crises going on that half the time you would never know you were in one.

But in Washington crises are built up slowly and dramatically. First, I know something is going on. I don't know what it is and my next-door neighbor has been sworn not to tell me. But I know he knows, and that's pretty spooky right there. Then I hear that something important is going to be done about something I don't know is happening. Key figures in government don't show up for dinner. Other key figures do show up for dinner. This is to confuse everyone. The Head of State catches a cold, the Vice-President catches a cold, the entire Cabinet is sneezing. It's safe to say when the President catches a cold, Cuba gets pneumonia. But that's all I know.

A newspaper friend calls up and says, "What do you know?"

You reply, "What do you know?"

He says, "I know it's big."

You say, "I hear it's tremendous."

"Who did you hear it from?" he wants to know.

"I can't tell you."

"That's the same guy I heard it from," he says. "I just wanted confirmation."

By this time your nerves are worn to a frazzle. Your wife wants to know if she can have new closets built. You tell her to wait until the President speaks. Finally the President speaks and you tell her she can't have her new closets. Then you have a crisis at home.

The main difference between a crisis in Paris and a crisis in Washington is that if you're an American in Paris and the crisis is serious, you know that the American government will evacuate you. But if you're an American stationed in Washington and the crisis takes a turn for the worse, you can be sure that nobody cares what the hell happens to you.

The Washington Expert

THERE IS A CERTAIN AURA surrounding somebody who lives in Washington. For some reason, everybody assumes you know more about what is going on than they do, and a fellow who makes his home in the nation's capital can eat and drink for nothing in most parts of the country, just on the basis of his living in Washington.

I discovered this when I went up to New York recently and found myself being invited out to a series of luncheons and dinner parties. Everyone was most interested in what was going on in Washington, and at first I was quite honest and admitted I had no idea. But this not only disappointed the people I was dining with, it infuriated them. They couldn't believe I didn't know and assumed I was holding out on them.

At the first dinner party the hostess told me as I left, "We didn't expect you to tell us everything, but I see no reason why you have to protect the Administration."

I decided then and there I would have to come up with some inside information or else I would have to pay for my own meals in New York.

So the next morning I bought copies of *Time, Newsweek, U. S. News and World Report,* and *The Nation* to read up on what was going on in Washington. Fortunately, the dinner party was late so I also had a chance to watch David Brinkley and Walter Cronkite on television. As an added measure of safety I stuffed a Walter Lippmann column in my tuxedo.

Nobody was better prepared to discuss Washington than I was.

"Tell me, sir," a distinguished banker said at cocktails, "what do they think in Washington about the Cuban situation?"

"We intend to remain firm," I said, as I popped an olive into my mouth.

"What do they say about taxes down there?" a distinguished lawyer demanded.

"There will probably be a tax cut in 1963," I proffered, as I stared at my ice cubes.

"You see, Helen," a doctor said to his wife, "the papers don't tell you that."

Helen replied, "He seems so young to know so much."

"My good man," an elderly broker said, "I heard a rumor that President Kennedy wanted to sell his plane, the *Caroline*, for $350,000. Is there any truth to it?"

I had to think fast as I hadn't read anything about it. "Yes, it's true," I said. "But the Republicans were the only ones who wanted to buy it. They didn't want to fly it, they just wanted to tear the wings off it."

"Can you tell us what the President plans to do about Berlin?"

"I'm sorry," I said. "There are some things the President discusses with me that I just can't talk about in public."

"Quite true," the lawyer agreed. "No sense tipping our hands to the Russians, and, after all, you have told us more than you probably should anyway."

I smiled indulgently. "I believe in a well-informed public."

The hostess made me sit on her right, and for the next three days I had more invitations than I could accept. But it's been quite a strain. I have to keep reading so many newspapers and watching so many television shows from Washington that sometimes I wonder if it's worth it.

Washington Parties Are Very Revealing

EVER SINCE I MOVED to Washington I've been reading the society pages with interest. The Washington society pages are different from any others in the world and most people turn to them before they read the front pages. The reason for this is that the hard news about world events is oftentimes buried in paragraphs devoted to embassy receptions, official dinners, and New Frontier cocktail parties.

This is how a typical Washington society-page story might sound:

"The Russians threw a wonderful party at their embassy last night to celebrate the arrival of the Bolshoi Ballet. In the receiving line was First Secretary Karnonsky, who with his lovely wife, Zina, greeted the guests. Zina told me she was sorry the Ambassador couldn't be there, but he had been called over to the White House for important conferences with the President. When I asked Zina where the Ambassador's wife was, she replied, 'She's packing the Ambassador's bag for a trip to Cuba.'

"I was very disappointed, as I enjoy talking to the Ambassador so much. But despite their absence, the table was loaded with caviar and smoked sturgeon and there was a lovely centerpiece of flowers which were arranged to look like an ICBM missile. Zina can do wonders with flowers.

"In the main salon I met General Werick Jablonsky, the handsome Polish military attaché, and his beautiful wife, Minka. Werick was telling some funny stories about Berlin and when I asked him if he thought Russia would sign a pact with East Germany, he handed me a glass of champagne and said, 'It's quite possible.' Minka was wearing a stunning blue dress and a blue hat with a veil to match. She always seems to have a nice word for everybody.

"I met Mrs. Nganda Ula, wife of the Congolese Minister for Economic Affairs, who said her husband could not be there as he was being held prisoner by the Katangans. Mrs. Ula was wearing an Indian sari of gold threads interwoven with pink and she looked striking.

"I was about to ask her how she was doing with her house-hunting when Colonel Singh of the Indian Military Mission and his wife greeted me. I hadn't seen them since Jackie Kennedy's visit to New Delhi. The Singhs made me promise to come to a dinner party they were giving for Prime Minister Nehru, who was coming on a secret mission to see President Kennedy.

"General and Mrs. Birch of the British Embassy told me it looked as though Britain would soon join the Cuban embargo. But what I really wanted to know was where Mrs. Birch got her beautiful beaded bag. 'That,' she said, 'is a military secret.'

"Charley Graham, of the Bureau of Standards, told me about a new drug which would cure the common cold, but I only listened with half an ear as I was so taken with Flora Graham's latest hair-do. It was a bouffant behind the ears with a daring flip. When Flora is with Charley, no one pays any attention to what he has to say.

"Major Hang Po, of Nationalist China, told me an amusing story about Quemoy and Matsu. He also revealed he was being relieved to take over a squadron of F-104s and I was sorry to hear it as Major Po is so well liked in Washington circles and supports all the charities in town.

"It was a wonderful party and would probably have gone on all night if someone hadn't shot the Bengonian Chargé d'Affaires. I had to go off to the Swedish Embassy for a candlelight dinner, so I never did find out who did it."

The Kennedy Industry

I MAY BE sticking my neck out very early but I'm predicting a landslide victory for President Kennedy in the 1964 election. It's not a question of politics, foreign policy, or his record in his first four years in the White House. It's purely a question of economics.

This is how I see it. In the beginning the Kennedys were a family. Then they became a political society. But now they've become an industry. And it's very hard to vote an industry out of office.

The Kennedy family inadvertently is providing work for hundreds of thousands of people throughout the country. There are people putting out JFK coloring books, photo albums, magazines, and copies of the *Mona Lisa*. There are Kennedy ash trays, post cards, neckties, and sweat shirts.

Every record company is fighting to duplicate Vaughn Meader's record of the Kennedy family. Thousands of television and night-club gag writers and performers owe their living to the Kennedys.

The fashion industry is dependent on Jacqueline Kennedy's dresses, the hairdressers are working overtime duplicating her hair style. She has given a boost to the water-skiing industry, and her vacations in Europe have helped the sale of airline tickets.

Fox-hunting equipment has never moved better. Horseback-riding stables are thriving. The Bobby Kennedys have put fresh water into swimming pools.

The decorating industry received a jab in the arm from Mrs. Kennedy's White House changes. Art galleries got a new lease on life. Robert Frost poems started to sell, Pablo Casals' record sales jumped, Ian Fleming's books made the best-seller lists.

The toy industry is thriving on Caroline Kennedy toys, the

pony breeders are getting rich on Macaroni. Touch football has come into its own. Rocking-chair companies can't fill their orders.

All this points to one thing. As time goes on the by-products of the Kennedy family will be responsible for millions and millions of jobs. Half the country will soon be employed in some way on Kennedy-inspired items. If things keep moving along the way they have been, the Kennedy family could become the biggest industry in the nation.

With so many people dependent on the Kennedys staying in the White House for their livelihood, I can't see how the President could lose. These people, no matter what their political convictions, will have to vote for him to preserve their jobs.

And the Kennedy industry has hardly been tapped yet. Just wait until Caroline becomes a teen-ager.

Calories Don't Vote

WHEN THE President of the United States told his press secretary, Pierre Salinger, to take a walk, he made one of the biggest mistakes of his political career. The President, who with the rest of the Kennedy clan is a bug on physical fitness, has not only challenged the size and shape of Mr. Salinger, but every American male who looks anything like him.

To many of us who weigh in about the same as Mr. Salinger, give or take ten pounds, he has always appeared to have the perfect American physique. His plucky figure, his modest jowls, his double chin were envied by all of us who felt that the stringy, lean and hungry look of the Kennedys gave the wrong image of a prosperous capitalist society on the move.

We who carry the breadbaskets of America around with us, under our belts, have always believed that exercise in any form was very dangerous for the human body. Doctors

will tell you that a person is born with just so much exercise in him, and if he uses it up when he is young, there won't be any left for him in waning years when he needs it the most. Therefore I believe one should conserve every ounce of energy, particularly in one's prime. I am not interested if Pierre Salinger can walk fifty miles today. I want to know if he can do it when he's seventy.

It seems to me that President Kennedy's physical fitness program and his demand that his people take long hikes has been inspired by political expediency. The one thing the people are concerned about is a healthy economy. President Kennedy wants to say to the American people, "If I don't produce a healthy economy at least I'll give you healthy economists."

But this physical fitness program could become a dangerous weapon in the hands of the executive branch of government.

Suppose the President wanted one of his Cabinet members to resign. In the old days, one of his staff would call up the *Saturday Evening Post* and ask to speak to Stewart Alsop or Charlie Bartlett. But now all the President has to do, if he really is determined to force someone's resignation, is to call up and say, "Adlai, I wonder if you'd mind taking a hike up to Poughkeepsie this afternoon along the Hudson River."

I'm not saying the President was trying to force Mr. Salinger's resignation by making him take that hike, but Las Vegas bookies were laying 8 to 5 that if Mr. Salinger did more than ten miles he'd be giving his press briefings in a wheel chair for the rest of the presidential term.

Politicians are loath to admit it, but there is a corpulent vote in the United States and many rotund voters are resentful over the way the President is treating his press secretary.

The corpulent voters of America, when they cast their ballot for Mr. Kennedy in 1960, did so because of Mr. Salinger. They felt that Mr. Salinger would represent their interests and would lobby for higher cholesterol quotas and Federal aid to the whipped-cream dessert industry.

But if the President is going to cut down on Mr. Salinger's

intake and make him hike in the bargain, he's going to lose the bulk of the American bulk voters.

We like Salinger just as he is. When Salinger waddles, we waddle with him; when he huffs and puffs, we know how he feels. There is no one in the Kennedy Administration that we identify with as much as the happy-go-lucky, cigar-chewing, balcony-prone press secretary, and if the President does anything to harm him Mr. Kennedy will lose the support of every Metrecal-hating anti-exercise constituent in the country.

Remember, Mr. President: Calories don't vote.

Nonphysical Fitness Has Lots of Heroes

I WAS GRATEFUL to receive such a warm response from people who had read my defense of Pierre Salinger. I was so heartened by it that I started an organization for nonphysical fitness titled, "Les Amis de Pierre Salinger" (The Friends of Pierre Salinger).

The object of the society is to discourage physical fitness in all its forms. Our motto is "Better Fed Than Red," and our colors are the same as that of a strawberry cheesecake.

Les Amis de Pierre Salinger is devoted to the American principles of life, liberty, and the pursuit of happiness providing there is available transportation to pursue it.

I can only sum up my philosophy by telling the story of a Rolls-Royce that pulled up at a fancy hotel. The chauffeur and footman lifted a fourteen-year-old boy out of the car and started to carry him into the lobby.

One of the guests went up to the lady and said, "What's the matter with your son. Can't he walk?"

The woman said huffily, "Why should he walk?"

Well, that's the way it is with Les Amis de Pierre Salinger.

We're ready to go anywhere our country needs us providing we don't have to go by foot. Thanks to Pierre, the National Council on Physical Fitness supports our attitude and says if you're not in condition to take a hike you can still fight communism by making a contribution to Radio Free Europe.

While Theodore Roosevelt is a hero to all the physical fitness nuts, we nonphysical fitness addicts worship at the shrine of Calvin Coolidge. Calvin Coolidge first expressed himself on this subject when he told the American people, "I do not choose to run."

Coolidge was noted for taking three-hour naps in the afternoon and not once in his career, as far as I know, did he order a Marine to take a fifty-mile hike.

As a matter of fact, a recent paper was found, purporting to have been written by Coolidge himself, in which he set down a test for nonphysical fitness experts. This test, with a few modifications, can still be tried by anybody.

The first part of the test is to go out in the woods and find a stretch of grass, spread out a blanket, and remain horizontally on it for no less than four hours. Then sit up and eat lunch for an hour. You have to be able to do twenty push-ups in this position, that is to say, you have to be able to push up the Thermos cup to your lips twenty times. Then you must turn over on the blanket on your stomach and remain that way for another four hours. Anyone who can complete the test will be given a certificate certifying his nonphysical fitness.

The Calvin Coolidge paper incidentally was turned over to President Kennedy. But because of his interest in physical fitness, he refused to release it to the public. It was leaked to us by a White House aide who shall remain nameless. Salinger may be plucky, but he's not stupid.

The President's Special Representative

EVERY ADMINISTRATION has a certain number of people who were appointed to high posts for political reasons. Although their value politically is finished, they could become more of a problem if they were publicly fired than if they were allowed to remain in the Government doing nothing. The Kennedy Administration is no exception, and so dotted all over Washington in great paneled offices, watched by one lonely secretary, are men who, having refused to resign, now sit guarding nobody's destiny but their own.

I was very grateful to have an exclusive interview with one such person, the President's Special Representative in Charge of Unemployment Problems in the Antarctic.

"Sir, I'm very grateful for this interview," I said.

"Don't be silly. I'm always happy to squeeze a member of the fourth estate into my busy schedule. Miss Bryan, please don't put any calls through for the next three hours."

"You haven't had any calls for three days," Miss Bryan said.

"Never mind," the PSR said irritably. "Now, young man, what did you want to know?"

"How often do you get to see the President as a Special Representative, sir?"

"At least once a month. The President is very concerned about unemployment in the Antarctic and he needed someone he could trust to do the job. I find the work so much more interesting than a Cabinet appointment and I have a great deal more room in which to maneuver."

"But what do you do for the President?"

"I can't tell you everything I do because the work is very confidential and encompasses so much more than just unemployment in the Antarctic."

"What else, for example?"

"Well, I'm in charge of employment in the Antarctic as well. I am chairman of a study group which concerns itself with ways of using the natural resources of the Antarctic for peaceful means."

"Have you made a study of the problem yet?"

"We're in the process of completing it now. I've had to make three trips to the Antarctic this year and I'm planning to go down again as soon as the ice melts."

"Does the President mind your being away so long?"

"No, on the contrary, he's encouraged me to make as many trips as possible. Every time I see him he asks me, 'When are you going to the Antarctic again?' Obviously he can't go and he needs someone he has confidence in. He's left instructions that any time I want to go to the Antarctic I can use his plane. Of course, I have to come back by boat, but I'm on per diem, so it all helps."

"What else do you do as the President's Special Representative?"

"Oh, lots of things. I picked up an honorary degree at the University of Pinball the other day; I addressed the Ladies' Auxiliary of the Auxiliary Firemen of Haverstraw, Nebraska; I threw out the first ball at a Little League game in Whapping, Arizona; and the next week I'm crowning the Ravioli Queen of West Tennessee. These are all jobs the President would like to do but can't."

"It sounds like interesting work. I understand there is a great deal of throat-cutting going on in the Administration. How do you get a job like this?"

"It's not easy. First you make a few speeches criticizing Administration foreign policy. Then you write a few articles for magazines telling how it is to work for President Kennedy, and then you release a story to the press that you're going to be fired. The President is then obligated to find a job for you. If there are no ambassadorships open, you automatically become a Presidential Special Representative at no loss in pay."

The phone rang, and Miss Bryan interrupted.

"I told you I didn't want to be disturbed."

"I'm sorry, sir. It's the White House calling."

"Oh, what do they want?"

"They want to know if you still want all that White House stationery you ordered?"

"Of course I do. How am I supposed to get the job done if I don't have the tools to work with?"

The Making of a Conservative

ACCORDING TO Senator Barry Goldwater there is a grass-roots movement towards conservatism that is sweeping the country. Since we always like to get on the bandwagon early, we dashed over to the Statler Hilton the other day to attend a convention of arch-conservatives and right-wing fellow travelers, sponsored by *Human Events*, a weekly newspaper devoted to fighting Communism, Socialism, New Frontierism, Liberal Republicanism, Governor Rockefellerism, and the United States Supreme Court.

We went up to the registration desk on the mezzanine floor and told the man: "Sir, I've been swept up by the grass-roots movement and I'd like to become a conservative. How do I go about it?"

He pinned a Barry-Goldwater-for-President button on our necktie and replied, "I'll have to ask you some questions first, to see if you're one of us."

"Yes, sir. Ask anything you want. You won't catch me taking the Fifth Amendment."

"Good. How do you feel about the Federal income tax?"

"Lousy. I think it's a scheme by left wingers in the government to make us pay for socialistic projects such as urban renewal, old age pensions, unemployment insurance, Federal education, and welfare payments for illegitimate children. If I had my way I would take the money I paid in income taxes and invest it in the stock market, where it belongs."

"Now let me ask you this. Where do you stand on nuclear disarmament?"

"I'm against it. I think we should not only continue testing, but we should drop a few bombs on other countries to show the Russians we mean business."

"Very good. What about desegregation?"

"I think desegregation is a Communist conspiracy to mongrelize the races, and a violation of the Tenth Amendment of the United States."

"What do you think of Bobby Kennedy?"

"Boooooooo."

"How do you feel about the Supreme Court?"

"They should all be impeached," we said. "I say take the prayers out of the churches and put them back in the schools, where they belong."

"Where do you stand on the United Nations?"

"The United Nations is a Communist organization with the specific purpose of keeping us out of war. I think U Thant should be impeached and the United Nations building should be turned over to Conrad Hilton for a new hotel."

"You seem to be doing very well," the man said.

"Yes, sir. I'm not trying to become a conservative for laughs."

"Let me ask this question. What is your personal opinion of Dwight Eisenhower?"

"He was a good general but when he became President he became a Communist and sold us out to the Russians."

"Why do you say he was a good general?" the man said suspiciously.

"I must have lost my head," we cried.

But it was too late. The man took back the Barry-Goldwater-for-President button and showed us to the elevator.

"For a moment there," he said, "I thought you were one of us. But you gave yourself away."

"Give me another chance," we begged.

He shook his head.

"We're a grass-roots movement and we can't afford to take chances with Eisenhower lovers like you."

Too Much Tittle-tattle

I HAD LUNCH with my good friend Peter Cook, one of the four stars of the British smash hit, *Beyond the Fringe,* when it was just winding up a successful run in Washington.

"How do you like Washington?" I asked him.

"It's rather terrifying," Mr. Cook said. "I keep going to cocktail parties and meeting people who seem to have their fingers on 'the button' or very near it. The British keep their button-pushers much more in the background. I suppose if I came face to face with a British button-pusher, he might be even less impressive than an American one."

Mr. Cook attended his first presidential press conference while he was in Washington and he commented, "The questions were so bad, you couldn't expect the answers to be very good. But I was very impressed by the up-and-down movement of the newsmen, who were never quite sure when President Kennedy would finish a sentence. The President has a beautifully modulated voice and uses such an endless stream of phrases that nobody can be certain when he's going to stop. Once he's in a sentence, it's very difficult for him to emerge from it. But I must say, your President is much kinder than Mr. Macmillan. When Mr. Macmillan is asked stupid questions, he's brief to the point of rudeness. Your fellow seems most amiable about answering anything."

My friend said that one of the things that struck him on arrival in the United States was that a stranger is subjected to a continuous stream of rumor and suggestion about the President. "I've never heard so much tittle-tattle about a head of state and his family as I've heard here. It's in total contrast to England where it's almost impossible to hear about Harold Macmillan."

Mr. Cook was also interested in the White House's culture program. "I suppose it's all right," he said. "The American approach to culture seems to be to give it snob appeal. If you show that the President takes a lively interest in the arts, even to the extent of importing them for his own living room, you may persuade the people to go out and see some. During the Eisenhower Administration the healthy American said, 'I wouldn't have Robert Frost in my living room.' Now thanks to Mrs. Kennedy, the healthy American, or at least his wife, says, 'Call up Pablo Casals and see if he can have dinner with us.'"

As far as his own show goes, Mr. Cook said that there are two subjects that Americans don't seem to find funny. One is God and the other is Cuba. "For different reasons, of course. The English don't mind our making fun of religion, but here you hit a stone wall on the subject. As for Cuba, the Americans are taking it far more personally than we took Suez. We're having an awful time with our Cuba jokes."

When it comes to day-to-day life in America, Mr. Cook said he was enjoying it. "I do get nervous when I hear the world news on the radio has been brought to me by a tissue company. We feel in Britain the news should be brought to you on its own without help from anybody."

One other gripe Mr. Cook has is that American restaurants are so mean with their butter. "Is butter really so expensive here?" he asked me. "All I seem to be able to get is one pat with every meal. It's most annoying, particularly since I like to put dollops on my bread. Everyone gets so resentful when I ask for more."

Mutiny at the Pentagon

THE GOOD SHIP Pentagon was almost rocked by a mutiny when a Navy captain named "Buzz" Lloyd decided to challenge Pentagon regulations regarding the parking of cars in the parking space reserved for small automobiles.

I was invited by the fighting captain to attend his trial

in the Pentagon traffic court where he was accused of parking his 1950 Chrysler in the small-car parking space. Captain Lloyd had deliberately parked his car in this space, because he felt that the Pentagon was discriminating against American cars.

Apparently the only space which is never filled in the morning, according to the captain, is the small-car parking lot. Therefore, the captain maintains, the Pentagon is unwittingly encouraging the flow of gold out of the United States by forcing military officers to buy foreign cars so they can have a place to park. Rather than pay his fine, he decided to go to court and make a plea for the American automobile.

When I arrived in the courtroom with the captain, I found it was already crowded with lieutenants, commanders, colonels, and civilians, waiting to face the Federal Traffic Commissioner. All these officers, in charge of moving thousands of troops, ships, planes, and supplies, had parked in the wrong place around the Pentagon building, and had to appear in front of the commissioner. Most of them pleaded guilty and were fined two dollars. Those who pleaded not guilty were asked to wait.

Captain Lloyd had brought a photograph of the parking lot with him. Since he was the only one who looked as though he was going to fight, his case was put last on the docket. While we were waiting, I offered him two steel balls to play with, but he refused them, fearing that if the judge saw them it would prejudice the case.

Finally he was called before the bench. Standing ramrod stiff in the best naval tradition, the captain faced the judge. His accuser, a Pentagon policeman, stood a little to the side, a receipt for the parking ticket clutched in his hand.

"How do you plead?" the commissioner asked.

"Not guilty," the captain said.

The patrolman gave evidence that he did ticket the Chrysler which he found in the small-car parking lot.

Captain Lloyd did not deny the charge. But, clutching the photograph of the Pentagon lot, he made an impassioned plea against the small-car parking lot. He pointed out that no American small car, with the possible exception of the Metropolitan, could fit the specifications of what the Pentagon had designated a small car. A car had to be less than 160 inches in length and 61 inches in width. The Falcon, the Corvair, the American, the Rambler, and the Valiant could not be considered small cars by this rule. He said the small-car parking lot was full of Volkswagens, Renaults, Simcas, Fiats, and MGs. He told of attempts to stop the gold flow and cited the President's "Buy American" program. He pointed out in the photograph that there was always room for foreign cars in the Pentagon parking lot, but none for American cars.

The judge studied Captain Lloyd's photograph carefully and he listened attentively to the captain's speech. Occasionally he made a note and finally, when the captain, fighting the greatest military battle of his career, finished, the judge said, "Thank you. I fine you two dollars."

Captain Lloyd was told that if he still wanted to fight the small-car principle, he should park his car in the small-car parking area, only this time when he got a ticket he should take his case to the United States District Court in Alexandria. The commissioner said he had no authority to rule on what constituted a small car at the Pentagon.

In checking with the Pentagon later, a spokesman for the parking lot said that the Pentagon was not discriminating against American cars. The trouble was nobody in America was making a really small car and the Pentagon could park five foreign cars to three American cars in the same amount of space. It was better to have a small-car parking lot so the foreign cars, which now number about two thousand at the Pentagon, did not take up large-car parking spots.

The captain paid his two dollars and, looking like Billy Mitchell after his court-martial, left the room.

I will always remember his words as we said good-bye. They were: "I regret I have only one Chrysler to give to my country."

Spying at the Pentagon

A BOOK WAS recently published titled *Spy in the U. S.* It was written by a Polish officer named Pawal Monat, who defected after successfully carrying out espionage against the United States. In the book, Mr. Monat said one of his best sources for loose talk about military subjects was the Pentagon, where he used to hang around in the halls and snack bars, picking up choice tidbits about military subjects. Eavesdropping at the Pentagon, according to Mr. Monat, is a must for all spies in Washington.

I decided to see if what the author-defector said was true, so I went over to the Pentagon in my best spy clothes and pretended I was in the pay of a foreign government.

There are 30,000 employees in the Pentagon, ten snack bars, six cafeterias, and seventeen miles of hall. So the problem for a spy is not how he can spy, but where to do it.

I started off at the snack bars, because it's very easy to stand close to someone in a Pentagon snack bar without looking suspicious. And besides, if you do look like a spy, everyone assumes you're one of ours instead of one of theirs.

At the first snack bar I bought a cup of coffee and sidled up to two Air Force lieutenant-colonels who were deep in conversation. I heard one say to the other, "So I said to him, 'Why don't you buy your own cigarettes instead of always mooching them off me?' And he said, 'Sir, I can't afford them on a sergeant's pay.'"

"Good for you," said the other colonel. "We have to pay for our cigarettes, too."

It was a good start for a spy and showed there was dissension in the Air Force.

I moved down the bar and heard one captain say to a major, "I had a TDY to Cape C to take some DVs for an FAT which held up my PCS."

I decoded this in the Army library later and what the captain said was that he had temporary duty at Cape Canaveral, where he had to take some distinguished visitors to see a final assembly test and this held up his permanent change of station.

Most military people at the Pentagon talk in initials. This is not only to confuse spies, but also to confuse the other services.

I don't wish to give the impression that there isn't any security at the Pentagon. There is. For example, no spy could drink more than six cups of Pentagon coffee before he would turn green and give himself away. This is how most spies at the Pentagon are caught. Only American military personnel can drink the Pentagon coffee without visible effect.

As a matter of fact, after my fifth cup I decided to go to the men's washroom, and it's lucky I did. I heard one civilian, who was washing his hands, say to another, "It doesn't make any difference. We have a big enough deficit to justify the expenditure."

I hung around the men's room a few minutes, but I didn't hear anything else of importance except some nonsense about missile sites, a new nuclear submarine, and some new secret war games that were going to take place next year—all stuff you could read in any newspaper.

Well, it was getting time for lunch, and I wandered over to one of the cafeterias, where I stood in line behind two Navy captains who were complaining that the black shoes were trying to get appropriations away from the brown shoes. The black shoes, it turned out, were nonflying Navy officers, and the brown shoes were the naval aviation people.

After choosing a breaded veal cutlet, stewed tomatoes, and iced tea (standard spy fare), I sat next to a group of secretaries who were revealing many secrets, none, unfortunately, that had anything to do with military matters. But I am the only spy in Washington that knows the right henna for a secretary to use on her hair.

I made three more cafeterias before the breaded veal cutlets

started to react on me and I had to go back to the washroom. It was there I met another spy who asked me for fifty cents so he could have a hot plate of food.

"Doesn't your government supply you with lunch money?" I asked.

"They used to," he said sadly, "but they just cut the budget."

Pentagon Survival School

THE CONGRESSIONAL HEARINGS into the TFX fighter-plane contracts have caused a great deal of bitterness in the peaceful city of Washington, D. C. A famous Air Force memo was circulated in the Pentagon charging that investigators for the McClellan committee subject Air Force employees to "oral abuse and unprovoked emotional ranting." The questioning was so rough, according to the memo, that one man collapsed from nervous exhaustion and two others "showed signs of deep fatigue."

Secretary of the Air Force Eugene Zukert was quoted as saying, "I understand from reports of witnesses that the interrogation was severe by any standards."

Now I'm not so worried about the Air Force's being subjected to rough questioning by Senate investigators as much as I am by the reaction of the Air Force to the questioning. It's obvious that the Air Force personnel in the Pentagon have gone soft, and what they need is a tough survival training school so they won't break under pressure from "the enemy," which in this case is the Senate investigations committee.

According to the Geneva Convention, all an Air Force officer has to admit under questioning is his name, his rank, and his serial number. The fact that the men questioned under pressure gave more than that shows that they are not psychologically prepared for Senate committee interrogation.

I have always believed that a Red Cross representative

should be present when someone from the armed forces is being subjected to questioning by a Senate investigator, but in peacetime this is not always possible. Therefore, a survival school at the Pentagon is the only answer. Everyone working there should have to go through the course before they would be allowed to have contact with subcommittee investigators.

The first part of the curriculum would deal with physical fitness. Students would have to run from the Pentagon to the Senate cloakroom in twenty-five minutes or less. They would have to do a hundred push-ups in front of Senator Jackson of Washington, who is trying to get the TFX contract for the Boeing Company, and they must be able to jump over the heads of Secretary McNamara and Arthur Sylvester, his press chief, from a standing position.

After completing their physical fitness training program, the trainees would then have to submit to psychological "brainwashing techniques." The student would be placed in a room and "tortured" by instructors portraying enemy subcommittee investigators. The tortures might consist of reading to the pupil Senator Ellender's full report on his trip to Africa or making the student listen to records of Senator Dirksen's speeches. They would include questioning him on the merits of the Skybolt, and making him repeat over and over again why the Air Force should have the RS-70 bomber.

If the student could pass the "brainwashing course" without breaking down, he would be given a certificate permitting him to be subpoenaed by a Congressional committee. If he flunked the course he would be sent to Alaska to man a DEW line observation post.

Unless the Pentagon does something immediately to prevent its personnel from cracking under stress, they'll find themselves with hundreds of turncoats on their hands, many of whom will be so brainwashed that they'll vote for the very men who are investigating them.

IT TAKES A HEAP
OF LIVIN'

New Frontiers at Home

THOSE OF US WHO LIVE in Washington like to think in Congressional terms. For example, at the time of year when Congress is winding up its session, each one must examine his own Congressional record at home.

My wife, who is the chief executive in our house, tried to ram a lot of bills down my throat this year, but I managed to throw out some of the more ridiculous ones. She did get her trade bill passed, though, in spite of strong opposition from this committee. The trade bill provides that she can trade with whatever store she wants to without authorization from me. She was also given the power to float a loan on anything she couldn't pay for.

Despite the fact that she is noted for her deficit spending, she received authority to increase the household debt by $5,000. All attempts by the opposition failed when she filibustered for three days over an amendment I introduced which provided for a balanced budget.

The largest appropriations went for what she termed "defense items." These included orders to purchase new lamps, rugs, a dining-room set, and a sofa. Without them, she maintained, she would have no defense against her friends, who, according to her, were winning the fight for space.

She also managed to get through an aid-to-education bill which provided funds for our son to go to private school. Since I was already paying for aid to public schools, I insisted the added expenditure was a waste of this taxpaper's money. But she threatened to bottle up in committee a request I had made for a new television set if I didn't pass her bill.

My wife has been very concerned about unemployment in

the United States and therefore she asked for authority to employ a housekeeper, handyman, electrician, and plumber. When I protested that there weren't enough funds on hand to provide full employment for everybody, she said she would veto a bill I had introduced which would provide funds for someone to cut our lawn every week.

One of the biggest battles we had was over foreign aid. My wife insists on spending hundreds of dollars on wedding gifts, birthday presents, anniversary mementos, and Christmas cards. I maintain most of this money is wasted and thrown into the wastebaskets of America. Not only is our generosity not appreciated, I have the feeling people hate us more for giving them something for nothing.

But my wife's foreign-aid program is the cornerstone of her administration. She says that unless she provides her family and friends with aid, they will go Communist on us, and it's easier to buy their friendship than to fight them. In a compromise session I managed to cut one hundred dollars from the bill by making her promise not to send out any Christmas cards.

Against strong protests my wife managed to get through a farm-aid bill by increasing her orders of milk, butter, and vegetables.

She also established a Medicare program for the family which doubles the fees I have been paying to doctors in the past.

In another hard-fought battle she managed to get authority to withhold household expense money from my check before I receive it. This, she claimed, was one of the big loopholes in our internal revenue system.

While my wife could claim victories on these pieces of legislation, I defeated her on her attempt to buy a new fur coat, shoes for the children, and ballet lessons for the girls. These will be held over for the next session, which starts in January. In the meantime the outflow of gold in our house has reached an all-time high.

Where We Stand: At Home

A LOT OF PEOPLE are worried about the American economy and where it's going, but I for one am not. I just bought a house in Washington, D. C., and as far as I can see, there will be enough work in the housing industry to support every man, woman, and child in the United States for the next twenty years.

My house isn't an old house, nor is it a new house. It could be described as early Alben Barkley, particularly since he once lived in it when he was a United States Senator.

I paid a lot of money for this house, but it is exactly the kind of house my wife and I have always dreamed of. It has a nice lawn, a garden, eleven rooms, and has been freshly painted. The big attraction to us was that we didn't have to put any money into fixing it up and we could just move in, as it seemed to be in top-flight condition.

But two weeks after we moved in, I walked down into the cellar and noticed two drops of water on one of the walls. There seemed to be a leak in one of the windows, and so I called a handyman, whose name I found in the phone book, and asked him to repair the leak.

He took one look at the two drops of water and said, "You're going to have to waterproof your cellar. I don't do that kind of work, but I know a company that does."

I said, "You mean I have to waterproof the entire cellar just because of two drops of water?"

"Look, there's obviously water coming in the cellar, and if you don't waterproof it, the whole foundation of your house will collapse. You want that to happen?"

"Heavens, no," I cried. "Send over the waterproofing company."

Two days later, the estimator from the waterproofing company came and took one look at the cellar. "Hmmm," he said,

"I didn't realize it was this serious." He kept hitting his fist against walls. "Hmmm," he said, sticking his finger into a hole. "Hmmmm," he said, kicking the bricks. Finally, he took out a pad and pencil. "We'll have to do the inside and the outside. It will cost you six hundred dollars."

"For two drops of water?" I said.

"Two drops of water can make a house fall down."

We signed a contract.

"And by the way, I don't like your drainage on the outside of the house. You need one of your gutters repaired."

"Can't you do that?"

"No, we're only cellar waterproofers. But I know a company that will repair gutters. I'll call them for you."

A few days later, a man with a long ladder showed up with his helper and climbed up to the roof to repair the gutter. He climbed right back down again and said, "You need a new roof. The slate's all shot, and there is no sense of me fixing the gutters if your roof is no good."

"It looks perfectly good to me," I said, staring up at it.

"Sure, but some night it's going to fall in on your kids. Of course, if you don't mind the roof falling on your kids that's another matter."

"No, no, no," I said. "Give me a new roof."

"I'll put you in touch with a roofing company. After they put in the roof, I'll fix the gutters."

The roofing company came, and for only five hundred dollars repaired the roof. A few days later, the waterproofing company came, dug up all my shrubbery, and waterproofed the outside of the basement. Then, they did the inside. The two drops of water dried up, and I was happy I had had the work done.

Three weeks later, my wife said, "One of the bushes that the waterproofing company dug up doesn't seem to be growing. I called them, and they're sending over a landscape gardener to look at it."

On Saturday, the gardener showed up. "I'm going to have to replant all the bushes around the house," he said.

"Why?" I asked.

"Because they're too close to the waterproof paint. Do you want all the bushes to die?"

"Yes," I said. "We all have to go sometime."

"Don't listen to him," my wife said. "Replant the bushes. I don't want people to think we live in a pigpen."

"And while I'm at it, I don't like the looks of your lawn," he added.

"Yeh," I said. "And there are people that don't like Picasso."

"Hush up," my wife said. "Will it be very expensive?"

"I can do the bushes and the lawn for three hundred dollars."

"I could build a golf course for that," I protested.

"Suit yourself. But in six months, if you don't put in new sod, your house is going to look as if it's in the middle of the Sahara Desert."

My wife said, "Go ahead and do it."

While he was working on the bushes, my wife found a spider in one of the closets. She showed it to the gardener.

"You better get an exterminator. You start with spiders, and pretty soon you'll have all kinds of bugs. Might even have termites. Spiders like termites. I'll call my friend who is in the exterminating business."

The friend came over that night. "I don't like the look of that spider," he said.

"Who does?" I yelled.

"We better do the house from top to bottom, just to make sure."

After he was gone, I said to my wife, "Why didn't you just kill the spider without telling anyone?"

"You know I hate to kill anything," she said.

Three days later, after my wife prepared a particularly excellent meal, which I knew meant she had some bad news for me, she said, "The exterminator says we should line our closets with cedar, or the spiders will come back."

"And who is going to line the closets with cedar?"

"He has a friend," my wife said nervously. "He's bringing over the cedar tomorrow."

When the cedar liner was finished, he said, "You have an awful lot of exposed pipes in this house. One of them could break and damage all the stuff in your closets. You better have them covered up."

The cover-up man for pipes didn't like the electrical wiring. He had his friend come in and rewire the house. But the electrician noticed the fan on the oil burner wasn't working, and *his friend* came over to fix that.

The oil-burner man just told my wife he didn't like the looks of the boiler, and I'm waiting for the boiler man to show up tomorrow.

It has cost me twenty-five hundred dollars so far, not counting what the boiler man will find wrong when he arrives. Twenty-five hundred dollars for two lousy drops of water. Who says the American economy is in trouble?

Fine Arts Committee

THERE ARE MANY WAYS to furnish a house in Washington. After checking on some of the prices around, I decided to take a leaf from our First Lady and set up a Fine Arts Commission and ask for contributions from the American public.

The Chairman of the Fine Arts Committee, to furnish what friends have referred to as the Gray House, is my mother-in-law, Mrs. Paul McGarry of Warren, Pennsylvania. No furniture will be accepted until it has been photographed, authenticated, and approved by her. Also serving on the committee are the housewares manager of Sears Roebuck, the linoleum buyer at Montgomery Ward, the rug salesman at Woolworth's, and the art director of J. C. Penney's paint department.

The object of the committee is to appeal to the patriotism of the American people and ask them to contribute non-tax-

deductible gifts to preserve one of the most historic homes in Washington—as far as age goes, anyway.

Some of the gifts which the committee is searching for are a bed for our son's room, a desk and a lamp, and a wooden box for his toys. We also need a bed each for our daughters, or one large one which both of them could sleep in. My wife would like a double bed for the master bedroom in place of the place of the mattress we're sleeping on, and we could use a chair and sofa in the living room. She also mentioned something about a dining-room table and chairs, and we need some pictures, but only if they're framed, for the walls.

Unlike the White House, which has been picking and chosing carefully, we promise not to return any of the gifts. If we can't use them, we'll sell them, but the donor will still get credit and his name will be inscribed in a golden book which we also hope somebody will donate.

While our house is of a historical period, built somewhere between 1910 and 1915, the committee has wisely decided not to insist on furniture from that period. What we really could use is new stuff. Failing that, I will take anything that is more than a hundred years old.

The committee has already contacted the White House and told them we will take anything *their* Fine Arts Commission rejects. At this date this generous offer has not been acknowledged. I think the mistake was in sending the letter to Ravello.

Once the main pieces are donated, we will then accept other accessories such as lamps, rugs, end tables, a stove, and a refrigerator. A plaque will be put on the refrigerator giving the name of the donor and the name of the discount house where it was bought.

As far as paintings go, we will accept anything done by President Eisenhower or one of his assistants.

I also need a water sprinkler, a lawn mower, and a leaf rake. The committee will try to restore the lawn, but if this doesn't work, I may ask for donations of sod.

Every so often my wife will give a tour of the house, and give oral credit to the donors. The house will be open from

9:00 until 5:00 for visitors and in-laws. For further information you can write to my mother-in-law, who has decided to devote all her time to seeing that our house is worthy of her daughter's heritage.

The slogan of the committee is, "Just because you don't want to give it to the White House doesn't mean you have to throw it away."

A Thousand Dollars a Plate

As EVERYONE KNOWS, my family deficit for the year broke all records, and not only am I in debt, but my children and their children will be paying for my move back to the United States.

Once again the Kennedy family has saved me. After setting up our Fine Arts Committee to furnish our house and agreeing to take anything the White House rejected, contributions poured in from all over the land. But that still didn't take the place of money. Fortunately, my wife read in the newspaper that President Kennedy was raising money for the Democratic Party at a $1,000-a-plate dinner, followed by an all-star show at the Washington Armory.

"Why don't we have a $1,000-a-plate dinner at our house?" she suggested. "It would wipe out our deficit and there might be some money left over to buy a new rug."

"That's not a bad idea," I said. "How many people could we have?"

"Well, we could have eight at the dining-room table, but to make up all the deficit we should have at least twenty for a buffet and we would kill two birds with one stone. We owe dinners to so many people in this town that this would give us a chance to return their hospitality."

"But if we charged them a thousand dollars a plate, would we be off the hook with our friends?"

"I should think so. After all, we *are* giving them dinner."

"What can we serve for a thousand dollars?"

"I thought maybe chicken cacciatore, rice, salad, garlic bread, cheese, and coffee," she said.

"What about wine?"

"We could ask each person to bring a bottle. There is no sense in going overboard."

"You're probably right," I said. "We'll make it a buffet, but I'll hop around so no one feels cheated. Now that the menu is set, what can we do for entertainment?"

"We could play the Vaughn Meader record of *The First Family*," she said.

"Wonderful. And what else?"

"What about the Allan Sherman record, *My Son, the Folk Singer?*"

"Terrific. Playing both records in one night will really be a treat for our friends. Is there any chance of any live entertainment?"

"Jennifer could sing the new song she learned at school about a turtle."

"Then Connie will want to sing her song about the muskrat," I said.

"We'll let Joel do somersaults," my wife added. "He does them so well."

"Good. Now what about showing home movies of our last trip to Majorca?"

"And the day we took the family to the Bois de Boulogne and I got pictures of you falling into the lake."

"Of course," I said. "They'll certainly get their thousand dollars' worth, if it comes off as we plan."

"Well, I better start making up a guest list. Who can afford a thousand dollars to come to our house?"

"How about Jake the Barber for a start?"

The Big Questions

A FRIEND OF MINE wants to get married, but he doesn't know exactly what he wants in the way of a wife. Perhaps I can help him. It is no longer enough for a woman to be beautiful or a good mother or even a good cook.

When a man gets married these days, he must ask himself the following questions:

The first and most important one is "Does she have a driver's license?" No man can afford to marry a woman these days if she doesn't drive. When a bachelor is ready to settle down, one of the first things he is looking for is a chauffeur. He wants someone who can take him to and from the railroad station, a woman who can go to the supermarket alone, and take the kids to dancing school and the dentist. I've seen far too many marriages go on the rocks only because the husband has had to do the driving.

The second question he must ask himself is "Can my future bride keep books?" In today's society a woman who isn't a first-rate accountant doesn't deserve a husband. After all, a marriage is built on joint-income returns, monthly payment of bills, household budgeting, and charge accounts. There are bank loans and interest rates to be kept in order, clothing estimates to be submitted, doctors' fees to be balanced, and since a husband is much too busy to keep the books at home, he must find a woman who has a knack for figures. Who was it who said, "When the balance sheets don't balance at home, you can put love on the debit side?"

The next question he must ask himself, if he wants true happiness, is "Is she good with her hands?" Many marriages that start out wonderfully end up in the divorce courts because a woman is unable to fix something as simple as an oil burner or a garbage-disposal unit.

While it is essential that a wife be able to do all the household repairs, she should also have a flair for landscape gardening. There is nothing a man admires more in a wife than one who can grow flowers and cut the lawn. Show me a woman who likes to tear out crab grass and I'll show you a marriage that will last forever.

A man today needs a woman who is well drilled in athletics. "Will she be able to teach my son baseball?" a man must ask himself. "Does she know the fundamentals of football, swimming, and ice hockey? Can she discuss these things with me while I'm watching them on TV?"

If a woman scores on all the above points, then a man must ask himself, "How is she on packing my bags for a business trip? Is she strong enough to move furniture around without bothering me? Can she hang pictures straight? Is she the type to complain when she has to fix a flat tire? Can I count on her to shovel the snow out of the driveway?"

When a man asks himself all these questions and the answers are all in the affirmative, he can then go ahead and ask himself, "Do I really love her?" And if the answer is still yes, then I say what the hell, it's worth giving it a try.

Life Begins at Sixty

I READ IN THE PAPER the other day that a new pill may be on the market soon which would make it possible for a woman of sixty to have a baby. It seems that a Dr. Ringrose of Edmonton, Alberta, Canada, revealed it might be possible to develop a pill containing a hormone which would keep a woman fertile to a much more advanced age than ever before. How would a woman of sixty feel about this?

When I read about it I rushed to Brooklyn to see my Aunt Sadie and said, "Aunt Sadie, they've just invented a drug which makes it possible for a woman of your age to have a baby."

"Wash out your mouth with soap and water," she replied.

"I'm not kidding, Aunt Sadie. Just think—a woman of sixty can soon have a baby."

"If your Uncle Leo so much as lays a finger on me I'll hit him in the head with a chair."

"Aunt Sadie," I protested. "That isn't the way to behave. After all, America needs children, and if women of your age can provide them it will help this country tremendously, particularly in the cold war with China."

"It so happens I'm not interested in having any kids at my age, even if they give it to us free under Medicare."

"Why don't you want to have children now?"

"I'm tired."

"That's not enough of a reason," I said.

"It may not be enough of a reason for you, but it's enough of a reason for me."

"But just think of it. The patter of little feet around the house again, the cradle in the bedroom, the happy sounds of a baby crying for its mother."

"Listen Mr. Population Exploder, for twenty years I had my share of kids. I couldn't wait for your cousin Milton, and your cousin Ethel, and your cousin Leonard to go off and fend for themselves. I'm not ready to start on a new generation, even if they put the stuff in cereal boxes."

"I think you're wrong, Aunt Sadie. This is a new scientific development which could change the face of the globe. Women of your age will become important again. Advertising agencies will write copy about you. You'll be able to attend Parent-Teacher Association meetings. You can use your station wagon to bring kids home from school. Your grown-up children will have something in common with you if you have little children of your own. Retired people won't be considered expendable any more. What better way to fill out your final years than by producing babies?"

"Has your Uncle Leo heard about this?" she wanted to know.

"No, you're the first one I told."

"Well, if you tell him, I'll give you a hit in the head. We were just getting ready to enjoy the golden years after the sacrifice and work we had put in to raise our children, and now some baby-mad scientist in Canada wants to ruin everything."

"Then you're against the idea?" I asked her.

"You've come to the president of the Brooklyn Birth Control Society for Women over Sixty. Does that answer your question?"

"That's funny. I thought your reaction would be entirely different. Do you think most women of sixty feel this way?" I asked.

"You may get a different reaction from Elsa Maxwell, but I think I can speak for the rest of the country."

"Well, thanks for being so frank with me, anyway," I said.

"Don't mention it, and would you mind going out the back door? I think I just heard your Uncle Leo come in, and if it's all the same to you I don't want him to ask you what you've been doing here today."

French Phones Are Different

LIVING IN PARIS as I did for so many years, I've always had a built-in fear of the telephone company. The French telephone company can be very intimidating, not to mention the French telephone system as a whole. Therefore when my wife sent me down to the telephone company in Washington, D. C., to apply for a phone, I was quite frightened of the outcome. She packed me a lunch, as she always did when I went to the French telephone company, and gave me a clean shirt, a toothbrush, and a pair of socks. Sometimes it takes as much as three days to see the person in charge of getting a telephone in Paris, and we assumed the same thing would be true in Washington.

You can imagine my amazement when I was immediately ushered to the desk of an attractive woman and asked to sit down.

"I'd like a telephone," I said in the voice I always use for special pleading with French bureaucrats.

"How big is your house?" she asked kindly.

"We have eleven rooms, counting the basement."

"Then you'll need five telephones," she said.

"Five?"

"Yes. You'll need one in the kitchen."

"Of course."

"Then one in the living room," she said.

"But couldn't I use the one in the kitchen?"

"How could you if you were in the living room?"

"That's true. I hadn't thought of that," I apologized.

She forgave me and continued. "Then one in your bedroom on the second floor, one for your study, and then one on the third floor in the children's room."

"Okay, five phones," I said, trying to placate her.

"What color phones do you want?"

"I'll take one of each," I said, hoping to please her.

"Now of course you'll want the bell chimes."

"What bell chimes?"

"It calls you to the phone musically."

"I wouldn't have anything else in the house," I said. "Our whole family are music lovers."

"Very good," she said. "We have many other services, but I think this will be enough to start with."

"You mean I can really have a telephone?" I said, trying to hold back the tears.

"Of course you can," she said, wiping her own eyes with a handkerchief. "That's what we're here for."

I decided I had to leave before we both broke down.

As I ran for the door, she cried after me, "You left your lunch and clean shirt on my desk!"

The Problems of Being the Perfect Husband

I HATE TO ADMIT IT, but I'm the perfect husband. I'm not being conceited, nor am I necessarily bragging, because I know being the perfect husband is a God-given talent, and you're either born with it or you're not.

What makes a perfect husband? It's quite simple. The perfect husband is one who is able to see his wife's faults, correct them if they need correcting, show her what she is doing wrong, and at the same time do nothing to injure the relationship between the children and the father.

Marriage counselors will tell you that the happiest unions are those mixed marriages in which one of the mates is perfect and the other is not. Most marriages go on the rocks when both mates are perfect or both mates are imperfect. In my case I was just lucky to find an imperfect wife, and since I'm perfect we've had a very happy marriage.

It isn't easy to be the perfect husband. For one thing you have to be *right* all the time, and sometimes it's embarrassing when I constantly have to point out to my wife her mistakes.

Occasionally she gets exasperated and shouts, "If I could win an argument just once—that's all I ask, let me win one just once."

I would love her to win an argument, but how can I when she's always wrong. I could fake it, I guess, and pretend she was right, but then my image as the perfect husband might be tarnished and all discipline might break down between us. How can a wife respect a man who says she is right and he is wrong.

Let me cite some of the problems a perfect husband faces.

His wife has been at home all day with the children. Her nerves may be slightly frayed, her mental state might not be all one could hope for, and she keeps screaming, "Just wait until your father gets home." Now the perfect husband comes home. His role is that of a Supreme Court Justice. He must hear both sides of the case—his wife's as well as the children's. Since it is he who must mete out the punishment, he has to remain impartial and not let personalities get involved with the facts.

In many cases I've had to rule against my wife. She may have demanded that my son be sent to bed without his supper, or my daughter be forbidden to go ice skating with her friends. But after hearing the arguments, I've had to rule in favor of the children. Naturally my wife is disappointed and at the time she can even be angry, but in the long run I'm sure she realizes that as a perfect husband I had no choice. Since I'm also the perfect father I wouldn't want the children to think badly of me.

As the perfect husband, I have, on occasion, had to point out to my wife the faults in her relatives. Sometimes she feels the criticism is unjust, and probably from her imperfect viewpoint, she might really believe this is so. But I try to explain to her that she is blinded by familial love, and since I am not related to any of her people, it is easier for me to see what's wrong with them.

There have been moments when she has tried to point out imperfections in my family, but none of them have ever held up. I have the perfect family—otherwise how could I be the perfect husband?

If one is perfect in his home life he should also be perfect in his social life. At parties I am most flattering to the ladies and willing to listen to anything they want to tell me.

My wife has always felt that at a party I should pay more attention to her, and some of our fights have been over the attentions I have paid other women. It's hard for her to understand that since I am the perfect husband, I must be shared with others and she shouldn't be selfish about me. It is quite possible some of the women I talk to don't have perfect husbands of their own, and need a friendly ear or a sympathetic smile. But all my wife makes of it is that I'm flirting with another woman. The charge is so ridiculous I refuse to dignify it with an answer.

Some men think that to be a perfect husband they have to help around the house, cut the lawn, take out the garbage, clean the cellar, and repair the roof. This is nonsense. The perfect husband is not the one who does the chores, but the one who knows how to delegate authority and distribute the work. In order to be the perfect man you shouldn't get involved in work that is beneath you. Kings don't stand guard duty; presidents don't shovel snow; prime ministers never wash their own cars. If you're the perfect husband you must insist on dignity. Let the people with imperfections do the dirty work.

If you're married to the perfect man, you will probably recognize the traits in your own husband that I have pointed out. If you're not, aren't you sorry you're not married to the perfect husband?

The Servant Problem in the United States

WHEN WE MOVED from Paris, France, to Washington, D. C., everyone warned us that the one thing we would find different in the United States was the help situation. You can still find very good help in France and I'll have to admit we were spoiled. Our Danielle, whom we had to leave behind because she was going to marry our butcher, was a gem. She was in the kitchen at seven in the morning, cooked breakfast, cleaned the house, cooked lunch, did the laundry and pressing, cooked the children's dinner at six, and then served the grown-up dinner at 8:30. We made sure, unless we had a dinner party, that Danielle was in bed by 11:30 p.m., and we gave her one day off a week. It was no wonder she loved us and we loved her.

Well, when we moved to Washington we knew we would have to make a few adjustments as far as the help situation goes, but we didn't realize to what extent they would go.

The first person my wife hired was Hedda. I found Hedda very amiable and after meeting her I knew my friends had exaggerated the difficulties of finding American help.

Hedda lasted a week.

I came home one night and found my wife crying.

"I had to fire Hedda," she said.

"Why?"

"She took all of Joel's comic books."

"Well there's nothing wrong with that," I said. "We'll get Joel new comic books."

"But she read them all day long," my wife said, "except when she had coffee with me in the kitchen, or when she got a telephone call from her boy friend. I had to do all the work myself."

"Well, just call the agency and hire someone else."

My wife hired a Mrs. Murphy and she turned out to be a jewel. She cleaned upstairs and down, did the laundry, prepared the meals, and even offered to stay late when we entertained.

A week later I came home and found my wife crying.

"Don't tell me you fired Mrs. Murphy," I said.

"No, she quit."

"What on earth for?"

"We ran out of liquor."

"What's that got to do with it?"

"Mrs. Murphy was a lush. And out-and-out all-day drinker. She kept nipping at your bottles and when you ran out she decided there was no reason for her to stay any longer. She said it was the most unhospitable house she had ever worked in."

"Oh well, call the agency and get somebody else."

The next maid was Helena. She stayed for ten days, a record in Washington, D. C., we discovered later.

Helena said we lived too far from her home, and besides we

took social security out of her salary and any family that did an un-American thing like that didn't deserve a maid.

"You're hiring the wrong maids," I accused my wife.

"All right then," she said tearfully, "you hire the maid."

"I certainly will."

I called the agency and told them to send over the best maid they had. Then I told my wife to clean the house from top to bottom.

"What for?" she wanted to know.

"We don't want her to think she has to clean a dirty house, do we?"

"I guesss you're right," my wife said wearily. "Do I have to shampoo the rugs too?"

"I should hope so," I said, surprised she would even ask such a question.

The next morning, bright and early, Angelina arrived. I invited her to sit in the living room and told my wife to make her some coffee.

Angelina said we had a very nice house.

"I'm glad you like it," I said nervously.

"Do you have any references?" she asked me.

"Well, I have a letter from our French maid who was very pleased working for us. Unfortunately, it's in French."

"That's all right, I'll take your word for it." Angelina said. "What kind of a vacuum cleaner do you have?" she demanded.

I told her and she said, "I don't like that make. You'll have to buy another one."

"Of course I will," I promised. "Is there anything else?"

"I have to have Thursday off, because that's the day my French poodle gets clipped."

"Certainly."

"And no Saturdays or Sundays."

"I wouldn't think of it," I promised.

"Do you have a car?"

"No, but we'll get you one," I said.

"Good," said Angelina. "Well, we'll give it a try. If I have anything else I need I'll let you know."

"You see," I told my wife after she left. "It's just a question of how you treat them. And did you notice Angelina looked so much like Danielle?"

"No, I didn't," my wife said peevishly.

Things went along fine for three weeks and then one day my wife came into the kitchen and found me crying.

"What happened?"

"Angelina's quitting," I sobbed.

"Why?"

"She says she doesn't like the meal you've been cooking for her. She says either you go or she goes."

'What did you tell her?"

"I haven't given her an answer yet. Sit down, dear. There is something I would like to talk over with you."

The Guilt Makers

IF ANYONE was to ask me what gives an American the most pleasure, I would answer it was to make somebody else feel guilty. We all wallow in guilt and the most simple telephone call can send us into the depths of despair.

Here are some of the leading guilt makers in one's life. For obvious reasons I haven't identified who they are.

"Yes, son . . . It's nice talking to you. I'm always delighted to hear from you, even though you only call once a week . . . No, I'm not complaining. After all, you have your own life to lead, and I'm not one of those mothers who is always interfering . . . I have television and my friends stop in once in a while to visit me and I take nice long walks when the weather is good, though of course my health hasn't been the best in recent months . . . You wouldn't know about that, of course.

"How is everybody? . . . Yes, I'd love to come over some time, but I don't want to come if I'm not wanted . . . I know you want me to come over, but I have the feeling you're just asking me to be nice to me . . . I vowed when my children went away I wouldn't be a burden on them . . . After all, you don't need your mother any more. . . . Well, if you don't think I'll be in the way . . . You have all those swell friends and I'm sure they wouldn't want to talk to me . . . No, son, I'm not being ridiculous. . . . Yes, I'll come next Sunday. . . . Have you asked Marjorie? . . . Maybe she'd rather I come at another time . . . All right, but I don't want to be a burden. . . . I won't stay long, just to see the children and then I'll leave. . . . Will you stop shouting? . . . I don't know why you get mad at me every time you call."

The second one who always makes you feel guilty is:

"Hello, Harry . . . This is Johnny from P. S. 35 . . . I was wondering if you and your wife would like to come over to dinner next Friday. . . . Oh, you're busy. . . . Sure, sure I understand. You're a big man now and it's pretty hard for you to keep up with your old school buddies. . . . Heck, no, I'm not sore. . . . I'm proud of you. . . . After all, you're the only one from the gang who made it big. . . . It would have been nice to talk over old times, but I guess we better make it another time. . . . Irma told me not to call. She said she knew you'd be tied up. . . . Yeh, I'll call you some other time. . . . I'm grateful you returned my call. Irma said you wouldn't even do that."

The third guilt maker:

"Yes, dear . . . You have to go to Miami next week for the meeting . . . No, that's all right. . . . Of course I understand. . . . What do you mean can I go? You're being silly now. You know I can't leave the children. . . . I'm not angry . . . I've got some books I want to read and there's always television to watch . . . How long will you be gone? . . . Four days? . . . Good, I just wanted to know how many sleeping pills I'd need. . . . You know how badly I sleep when you're gone.

"I wish you would not keep protesting so. I know it's important. Everything you do is important. . . . Nothing I do seems to be very important. . . . Get the kids to school, clean the house, fix the stove, I think I'll become a housemaid . . . then at least I'd get paid for what I do.

"Of course I'm not bored . . . I just used a new detergent

today and it's changed my whole life, just as it says in the television commercials . . . My sheets are whiter, whiter, whiter, whiter, and wait until you touch my hands—they're so smooth, smooth, smooth.

"No, I haven't been drinking. . . . The Barnetts want us a week from Thursday for dinner. . . . You won't be in Chicago or Paris then will you? . . . I'm not being sarcastic, but I don't want to do anything to interfere with your work . . . You don't have to go to the Barnetts' on my account. After all, you did take me out last month . . .

"I wish you wouldn't keep using those words . . . The children may be listening in on the extension . . . Are you coming home for dinner tonight? . . . I just thought I'd ask . . . Maybe you had a business appointment or something . . . Good, I'll see you at six, but if something comes up don't worry about me, I've still got the crossword puzzle to do."

The final guilt maker is guess who?

"Hello, Daddy, when are you coming home from the office? . . . Are you and Mommy going out tonight? . . . You never stay at home . . . You're always going out . . . Are you going to bring a present? . . . You never buy me anything . . . Mommy won't let me stay up and watch television . . . You never let me do anything . . . I didn't hit Jennifer . . . She hit me first . . . You're always taking her side. . . . Nobody loves me . . . I wish I was an orphan . . . Nobody cares if I'm dead or alive. . . . Good-bye Daddy. I'll see you soon."

It's Simple To Cut a Mate Down to Size

I READ THAT a Swedish surgeon performed an operation on a man and shortened his height by six inches. Originally the man was seven feet seven inches tall, but after the operation he was seven feet one inch tall. Now this may be some sort of a milestone for medicine, but I know wives who have been cutting down their husbands for years and nobody says anything about it.

I have one particular friend who, when he got married stood six feet three inches. But after seven years of marriage he is now only five feet tall.

There are many ways of cutting a husband down to size. The easiest way to do it is at a dinner party just as a husband is about to tell a story. "Oh, Charles," the wife says, "you're not going to tell that tired old joke again, are you?" Lop! Off goes two inches.

Another way to do it is to say in front of all his friends: "George is the only one in the office who didn't get a bonus this year."

Some wives like to chop down their husbands on cultural matters. "The only thing Harry will watch on television is westerns. I don't think he's read a book in years."

"All John loves to do is drink beer and go to wrestling matches." While everyone at the party laughs, John gets smaller and smaller.

Some wives prefer to cut down their husbands in front of their children. I know one woman who, when her husband is trying to tell his children what a great football star he was in school, always says, "Hah, he sat on the bench for two seasons without playing a game."

Another wife waits for her husband to recount his war experiences to the family. Just when he's in the middle of a hair-raising tale of being caught behind German lines, she says, "Oh, for heaven's sakes, tell them the truth. You never got nearer to Germany than Fort Dix." This fellow, who once played basketball in college, is now a midget.

One method of shortening a husband is to remind him what the next-door neighbors have purchased. "Jane Lindsay has a new leopard coat. Of course, we couldn't afford anything like that on the salary you make. But then again Arthur Lindsay is so much more aggressive than you." Or: "The Aldington children are going to summer camp. I had to tell the children they couldn't go to camp because their father doesn't make enough money."

It's surprising how few men protest when their wives cut them down. You would think their feet would hurt, but I've seen men who, when they started out on a picnic, were ten feet tall, but after their wives got finished with them, they could barely crawl to the car.

I've been very lucky in my married life because I've only lost a couple of inches. Usually it happens when I'm expounding on some political subject and my wife says, "He really doesn't know what he's talking about."

Or when I'm in an argument with someone, my wife always seems to take the other side and says, "You may say that now—but that isn't what you said at home."

Usually when I go to parties where I think my wife is going to turn on me, I wear elevator shoes. Then when she cuts me down, all I lose is leather instead of bone.

Most serious operations on husbands take place in the morning after an all-out party the night before when the husband thought he was at his best. It is then that the wife says, "Did you make a fool of yourself last night! I was so embarrassed I wanted to cry."

After one of those post-party sessions, it's a wonder a husband can ever walk again.

Cutting Down to Size Can Work Both Ways

AFTER I WROTE about how women cut their husbands down to size, you can imagine my surprise when I received thousands—hundreds—well, at least twelve letters from indignant women who asked me why I didn't give the woman's side of the story.

"There may be cases," one woman wrote, "of wives cutting

their husbands down, but I know in my case it's my husband who has done the shortening. When I was married I stood five feet three inches. Now I have to stand on a box to cook the evening meal."

There are many methods of cutting a woman down, according to my correspondents. One of the favorites is for a husband to say at a dinner party: "Speaking about driving, do you want to hear what my dumb wife did the other day? Knocked over a parking meter. Ever heard of anyone knocking over a parking meter? Well, there she is."

Another method is to discuss one's wife's financial affairs: "Don't complain about your wife. You should see Nancy's household accounts. I swear if a CPA ever looked at them, we'd all go to jail." Or: "So I said to my wife the other day, 'Look, if you can't add two and two, let the kids do it. I didn't marry you for your brain.'" Or: "Honey, tell the folks how you were overdrawn at the bank and you insisted it was their mistake. Listen, folks, this is the funniest thing you've ever heard."

One woman wrote that her husband specializes in cutting her down at weddings. "Freddie, boy," he'll say, "you're crazy to get married. I was once a happy guy just like you and look at me now." Or: "I hope your wife turns out to be a better cook than mine did. Do you know we've been married fourteen years and she still can't boil a pot of water?"

Another woman said her husband prefers shortening her size at home, while they're entertaining. "Hey, honey, when's dinner going to be served? These folks are hungry and you invited them for eight o'clock." Or: "Don't mind my wife. She's queer about candles, but at least you can't see what you're eating." Or: "Helen did the whole place over all by herself—and a decorator. It cost me fifteen hundred bucks. Boy, did she get taken!"

Probably the easiest and best way to cut down a woman is to discuss her clothes. One woman says her husband is the world's expert. He will tell her, "I like that suit, dear. It's just like the one Esther Jennings wore at the club last Sunday, and Esther has real good taste." Or: "I don't care if you wear the black dress with the white collar or the white dress with the black collar. At your age nobody's going to notice anyway."

And so it goes. Husbands cutting down wives, wives cutting down husbands. It's a wonder the majority of people in the United States aren't midgets by now.

To make matters worse, when a husband isn't cutting down his wife and his wife isn't cutting down her husband, the kids are cutting down both of them. How many of us have heard our kids say, "Mommy and Daddy are okay, but they're not very bright"?

Unions in the Home

MY WIFE WAS very much influenced by the printers' strike in New York City, and she read so much about it that the idea occurred to her that there should be a housewives' union. She feels that one of the reasons American women are unhappy and the divorce rate is so high in the United States is because housewives are not organized, and are constantly being exploited by their husbands and children.

"What union would you belong to?" I asked her.

"The Teamsters Union," she replied. "If we're going to be treated like horses we might as well belong to Jimmy Hoffa."

In order to humor her, I agreed to open labor negotiations with her. But her demands were ridiculous. She wanted a seventy-five-hour workweek as opposed to the eighty-hour week she is working now. She demanded an increase of $13.00 a week for household expenses, and fringe benefits that would come to another $3.50 a week. She asked for two weeks' sick leave, one week's vacation with pay, and double time for Mother's Day. All in all, the demands she made would cost me an extra $37.00 a week, and I have no intention of agreeing to them.

I pointed out to her that the eighty-hour workweek for mothers was approved by the National Labor Relations Board and upheld by the United States Supreme Court. The increase in household expenses was not justified at this time, as it would only add to the inflationary spiral, as well as increase the deficit we were operating under at home.

Her demand for two weeks' sick leave was unrealistic. I have made provisions for her to be sick for one full week a year and that's plenty for any wife and mother.

As far as fringe benefits go, she is entitled to Family Blue Cross, and I promised never to dock her clothing allowance for any time, up to a week, that she has to spend in bed.

The question of a vacation is up for negotiation. I personally don't think a wife should have one, as it interrupts the flow of production, and only makes her more unhappy when she goes back to work. But I'm willing to have this point arbitrated by Mayor Wagner if the rest of the questions can be resolved.

One of the points where I cannot agree is automation. My wife wants the house fully automated to cut down on a great deal of hand labor. I refuse to give in on this point, not only because of the cost, but because if I install labor-saving devices it will be an open invitation for her to slow down in her work and encourage her to take coffee and smoking breaks.

Last year when I installed a washing machine, my wife used the leisure time to call her mother. I had to pay not only for the machine, but also for the added telephone calls caused by her being away from the scrubbing board.

Another point of real contention is job security. She wants it in writing that her job will be protected and that I won't hire someone to replace her if she makes mistakes. I told her I can't guarantee her job. As long as she cooks for the family and she has an efficiency rating of 4.0, she will have her position. If she falls down in her household work or neglects her duties, I must have the freedom to fire her. How else can a husband run a home?

This is where negotiations stand now. Neither side will give in. My wife says, "No contract, no featherbedding." It's enough to turn a man against unions for life.

Kid-swapping in the United States

NOBODY LIKES TO TALK about it, but there is a lot of kid-swapping going on in the United States. It isn't going on just in the suburbs or the small towns, but in the larger cities as well.

I hadn't realized how prevalent kid-swapping was until I moved to Washington. One night I came home from the office, and instead of finding my dark-haired little beauties, I discovered a seven-year-old blonde stranger doing the twist.

"Who's she?" I asked my wife.

"That's Ann Lindsay. She's staying here for the night with Connie."

"Where's Jennifer?" I asked.

"She's sleeping at Priscilla's house, because Ann Lindsay's sleeping here."

"Who's Priscilla?"

"Jennifer didn't know her last name, but she says she's her best friend."

"That's nice. Where is Joel?"

"He's sleeping at his friend's—B. J. He said if Jennifer can sleep somewhere else so can he."

"Where does that leave us?" I asked my wife.

"Well, we had three to start with, we got rid of two for the night, and we gained one, so we're only short one."

"It saves on food," I agreed.

"Not really," my wife said. "We had fish tonight, but Ann Lindsay doesn't like fish, so I had to go out and get her a steak. Then when Connie saw Ann was getting a steak she wanted one, too."

"I wouldn't mind having a steak myself," I said.

"You can't. Somebody's got to eat the fish."

The next weekend when I came home Connie was missing, but Jennifer had two friends and Joel had B. J.

At eight o'clock I ordered them all to bed.

"B. J.'s father lets him watch television until midnight every night," Joel, who is nine years old, said.

"Is that true, B. J.?" I asked.

"Sometimes later," B. J. said without batting an eye.

"When I stayed at B. J.'s last week," Joel said, "we didn't go to bed until two in the morning."

"My parents don't like me to go to bed early," B. J. said, "because then I wake up early."

"Well, why don't we just call up your parents and ask them what time you go to bed?"

"Oh, you don't have to do that," B. J. said hurriedly. "They've probably gone out to a movie."

Just then the phone rang. It was Mrs. Lindsay, who said, "What time do you usually put Connie to bed?"

"Eight o'clock," I said.

"She said you let her stay up till midnight to watch television. I was a little worried." Mrs. Lindsay seemed relieved.

Later that evening I said to my wife, "We've got to put a halt to this kid-swapping. Everyone on Cleveland Avenue is starting to talk."

"Oh, it's harmless," my wife said, "and they get so much fun out of it."

But I knew what I was talking about. A few weeks later I came home and found three kids at the dinner table. None of them mine.

"What happened?" I asked.

My wife was rather embarrassed. "There's been a dreadful mix-up. Joel invited Francis over to sleep with him, but he forgot he'd accepted an invitation to sleep at Butch's. Jennifer and Connie were invited over to Karen's, but after they left, Veronica and Mary Elisabeth showed up and said they had been invited over here. I didn't have the heart to send them home."

"So now we've got three kids that don't even belong to us," I said.

"Yes," my wife said, "and guess what? They said their

mothers let them stay up until midnight every night to watch television."

Household Fatigue

MANY HUSBANDS don't realize it but their wives are suffering from "household fatigue," a state similar to the battle fatigue of World War II, only more difficult to recognize. I probably would have never realized that my wife was a victim of it if I hadn't decided to take her with me to Cincinnati, where I had to make a speech. She seemed quite normal preparing for the trip and even appeared to be excited about getting away from the house for a few days. But then when we arrived at the airport I noticed her behavior had started to change.

As I paid for our airline tickets she said to the man behind the counter, "Just a minute. Where are our green stamps?"

"Madam, we don't give green stamps to our customers for using our airline."

"Is that so? Well, we'll just use another airline that does."

"Mother," I said, "none of the airlines gives green stamps and besides this is the only airline that goes to Cincinnati."

I calmed her down and thought nothing more of it until we got on the plane. The first thing she did was start to dust the seats.

"Mother, you don't have to do that," I said.

"I'm not going to have the neighbors think I keep a dirty plane."

"But they have people to do this sort of thing. Now sit by the window and fasten your safety belt."

I got her to sit down quietly and gave her a magazine to read. As soon as the plane was in the air she was up. "I've got to prepare lunch," she said.

"They have stewardesses to prepare lunch. You don't have to do anything."

"Well, I have to get the meat out of the freezer."

"No, no. That's all done by the airline personnel. You're on vacation. Relax."

She sat back for a few moments, but then one of the stewardesses spilled a cup of coffee in the aisle. My wife jumped up and said, "Don't worry about a thing." She took a container of Mr. Clean from her make-up kit and on her hands and knees worked on getting out the spot.

"There," she said after fifteen minutes, "Mr. Clean does everything."

Everybody looked away in embarrassment.

An hour later luncheon was served. There were two children sitting across the aisle from us, but they didn't seem to be eating their vegetables.

My wife looked over and shouted at them, "If I've told you kids once, I've told you a hundred times. You don't eat your vegetables, you don't get any dessert."

"Mother, Mother," I said gently, "those are not our children."

"I don't care," she said, "I'm sick and tired of preparing meals on this plane that nobody wants to eat."

"But maybe their parents don't want them to eat vegetables."

"You're always defending them," she said angrily. "No wonder they have such bad table manners. Sit up," she shouted at the little boy, "or you can go to bed right now."

Fortunately the parents of the children were preoccupied, and my wife decided to go back and help the stewardesses wash the dishes. By the time we reached Cincinnati, she had cleaned all the windows, washed the ash trays, laundered the napkins, and changed the curtains in the bar.

But the two days away from home have done her wonders. She hasn't yelled at any kids in twenty-four hours, and she's almost cured of her household fatigue. It's a pity she has to go home so soon.

Where Fathers Fear To Tread

ONE OF THE BIG PROBLEMS of having small daughters, for a father, is they always seem to have to go to the bathroom when their mother isn't around.

I took my two little girls, aged seven and six, ice skating at the Sheraton-Park Hotel. After they skated two or three times around the rink, they both announced that they were "cold" and wanted hot chocolate.

Then my youngest daughter said, "I have to go to the bathroom."

"Can't you wait until you get home?" I asked her nervously.

"No," she said. "I didn't even go at home before I left."

I sought out the bell captain. "I beg your pardon," I said. "Could you please tell me where the ladies' room is?"

"The men's room is downstairs," he said coldly.

"No, I don't want the men's room. I want the ladies' room."

He was just about to call the house detective and have me arrested when I explained it wasn't for me, it was for my daughter. "Okay," he said, "the ladies' room is down the hall on your right."

I dragged both children down the hall.

"You come in with me," my daughter said.

"I can't go in with you," I said, perspiring. "Connie will go in with you."

"I don't want her to go in with me."

"All right, go in by yourself, but come right out."

She came out in about ten seconds.

"That was fast," I said.

"I didn't go," she said.

"Why not?"

"You have to have a coin to get into the toilet."

"What kind of coin?"

"I don't know."

Having never been in a ladies' room, I gave her a quarter, a dime, a nickel, and a penny. "Here," I said, "try one of these."

She came out a minute later.

"Okay?"

"No," she said. "I didn't go."

"What happened?"

"I put in the quarter and then the dime and the nickel and the penny and nothing happened."

"The door wouldn't open?"

"No, it made a funny noise, but it was locked."

I gave her another quarter and a dime. "Put one in at a time," I told her. "But don't put them into the same one as you put the other coins."

I went back to my vigil at the door.

Every once in a while I shouted, "Just wait until you come out! Are you going to get a spanking!"

But every time I shouted someone seemed to walk by.

Finally Jennifer came out. I was just ready to whack her when she said, "I didn't go yet."

"Why not?" I gasped.

"The door won't open."

"I know what to do, Daddy," Connie said.

"You stay out of it!"

"Mommy makes us do it all the time."

"Do what?"

"Crawl under the door. Mommy never puts any money into the machine. Then when we're inside we open the door for her. She buys us a present with the money she saves."

"Okay, Jennifer, crawl under the door like you do for Mommy and I'll buy you a present."

Jennifer came out in a few minutes.

"Okay?" I asked.

"Yes. I crawled under the door. What are you going to buy me?"

"A diamond ring. What else?" I shouted.

The Prowler

I HAD A PROWLER at the house one night. I was sitting watching television with a friend, Richard Condon, a writer, when my nine-year-old son came downstairs and announced there was a man in the backyard.

My son does not make up too many stories for a nine-year-old, but one always has to be careful, and I questioned him at length as to how he saw him. I even went up to his room to check if he could see a prowler from his window and it turned out he could.

So I called the police, who dashed over in less than two minutes, and we all went outside looking for the prowler, to no avail.

Then the police questioned my son. "What did the man look like?"

"He had on glasses and was kind of fat," my son said.

"Did he have a hat?"

"Yes," said my son, "one just like that one." He pointed to Mr. Condon's hat.

"What color suit was he wearing?"

"Brown" was the reply.

"Did he have a coat on?"

"Yes, he had on a jacket."

The police wrote everything down and congratulated my son on his ability to describe someone so accurately.

"I've seen grownups," the patrolman said, "who couldn't do half as well."

Joel was very proud. We all praised him, gave him some apple pie, and sent him off to bed with his toy gun strapped to his waist. The rest of the evening we spent talking about the prowler—who he was, what he was doing, and whether he would return or not.

Mr. Condon, being a novelist, was particularly delighted with the evening. He saw it in terms of a plot for a great story and I was happy I could provide the entertainment. I must admit I also was excited about the events and felt as though I had just participated in *The Naked City*.

But the evening had to come to an end and I said farewell to my guest and went to bed. About a quarter of an hour later the doorbell rang. I answered the door and there stood two husky policemen. Between them, looking outraged, as if he were going to suffer apoplexy, was Richard Condon.

"What's happened?" I asked.

"Have you ever seen this man before?" one of the patrolmen asked.

"Yes. But, officer, this man is my friend. He was in my house tonight," I said.

The officer looked at his notes. "He fits the prowler's description perfectly."

Suddenly it dawned on all of us at the same time. Joel didn't want to admit to the police he couldn't describe the prowler he saw, so he described Condon.

"Well, there must be another fellow just like him in the neighborhood," the policeman said, winking at me.

Condon took the incident philosophically. "I was wondering how I was going to finish my story and now I know."

"How?"

"The family's friend gets picked up by the police by accident, and after the family squares it away with the police, the family's friend leaves the house and then goes next door and starts peeking in the window."

3.
ANYBODY FOR FISCAL TRAINING?

What To Do with the Tax Cut

THE PRESIDENT SAID in his 1963 State of the Union speech that he recommended an income-tax cut for the American people. The idea, as I understand it, is that if people were given a better break on their income taxes, they would spend more money, and this would help the economy and create more jobs, and make a more prosperous and happy America.

What would people do with the money they didn't have to pay in taxes? I took my own personal survey to see what Americans planned to do with their new-gotten gains.

The first person I talked to was my groceryman. "What do you plan to do with the money you'll gain in the tax cut?" I asked him.

"I'm going to pay my taxes," he said.

"I beg your pardon?"

"I never have enough money to pay my taxes at the end of the year. So if I get a tax break, I'll use the money to pay my taxes."

I saw a Western Union boy on the street and stopped him. "What do you plan to do with the money you save on taxes?" I asked him.

"I'll probably set up a scholarship at Harvard for poor boys who may never otherwise have an opportunity to work for Western Union and become as successful as I am."

I saw a little old lady hobbling toward me, and I asked her the same question.

"I'll use it as a down payment on a lifetime scholarship at my ballroom-dancing school. I won a scholarship for ten free lessons, but they told me I was so talented that I must continue or I'll forget everything they taught me."

My laundryman said he and his wife were in disagreement as to how to spend the three hundred dollars a year he'd save on taxes. "She wants to buy a house at Palm Beach near the Kennedys, but I thought I'd rather put the money into a Van Gogh."

I talked to a bitter Civil Service employee on my block. "The savings in taxes will allow me to attend three $100-a-plate dinners for the Democratic Party during the next year."

I put the question to an elderly man who was waiting for a bus.

He said, "Burrurb, blurrbburb."

I said I didn't understand him.

"Blurrrburb, burruburb," he repeated. Finally he took a pad and pencil and wrote down, "I'm going to get myself a set of new teeth."

Very few people I talked to seemed to want to pour the money back into the American economy. One Army officer said, "I think I'll buy a Volkswagen." A bus driver said, "My wife already spent it and it isn't even a law yet." A Republican told me, "I'm going to give it to the Republican Party to get *that family* out of the White House."

I spoke to a newspaperman who had been laid off during the printers' strike in New York City. He said, "It's too early to say, but I think I'd like to buy something to eat."

Interview with a Tax Expert

THERE HAS BEEN a lot of confusion about President Kennedy's tax-cut and tax-reform bills, and I was very fortunate the other day to speak to Professor Heinrich Babelmeir, who holds the Billie Sol Estes Chair of Taxation at the University of Pecos.

"Professor Babelmeir, many people are confused about President Kennedy's tax-cut proposals. Could you enlighten us about how they will effect the average taxpayer."

"Of course I can. If the plan goes through, the taxpayer will benefit as much as two hundred to a thousand dollars a year."

"That's good," I said.

"No, that's bad. Because the President is also calling for tax reforms, and if these reforms are put into effect the people may benefit only from fifty to two hundred dollars a year."

"That's bad," I agreed.

"No, that's good. Because if this money is put into circulation, it will help the economy, strengthen the employment picture, and stop the flow of gold out of the country."

"That's good."

"You call that good? There is talk there will be a deficit of twelve billion dollars."

"That's bad."

"Don't be too sure. We've got to increase our gross national product some way. The only way you can do this is to spend money."

"But if we spend money and we get into debt, won't they have to raise taxes next year?"

"Please don't say 'raise taxes.' The Government doesn't raise taxes; it reforms them."

"What exactly is tax reform?"

"Tax reform is when you take taxes off things that have been taxed in the past and put taxes on things that haven't been taxed before."

"Is that good?"

"Well, it's not bad. You see, if you had tax cuts without tax reforms, you would be *cutting* taxes. And the Government really can't afford to cut taxes at this time. If anything, the Government could use more taxes."

"But if the Government needs more money, why does it want to cut taxes?"

"To jazz up the economy, stupid. If everyone spends the money they save in taxes, then the Government can tax the people who made the money which was spent by the taxpayers. With the tax money in circulation, there will be more money available for taxes."

"That's good," I said.

"It's not that good. You see, if the Federal government cuts taxes, the States will probably raise them to take up the surplus.

So, instead of paying your money to the Federal government, you'll pay it to the State."

"Then that means the money that was supposed to be put in circulation for consumer goods will still go for taxes."

"What else?" Professor Babelmeir said.

"If the State taxes the people what the Federal government saves them, then how much will each family save by a Federal tax cut?"

"It's hard to say exactly. We think it will be in the neighborhood of fifty to seventy-five cents a year."

"Well, at least that's something."

"It would be except every city and town in the United States is planning to raise its taxes."

"It doesn't make sense," I said. "After city taxes, how much is left?"

"I'm not sure, but I wonder if you could lend me your tax cut for 1963? I have to make a phone call."

Ira of the IRS

THERE HAVE BEEN television shows based on practically every profession in the United States. Newspapermen, doctors, lawyers, psychiatrists, social workers, private detectives, and FBI men all have been depicted on TV. Everyone has ignored the Internal Revenue man, and yet to many of us he is the most important person in our lives.

To right the wrong, I have written a television show titled "Ira of the IRS," the story of a man and his relentless fight against expense-account padding.

The scene of the first show takes place in the IRS offices in New York City. In charge of the office is Mortimer Income. His young, eager assistant is Ira. The third person in the bureau is Kelly—cynical, gray-haired, but a good driver.

The phone rings.

Mortimer: "What? Where? At the Four Reasons? Okay."

He hangs up and says to Ira and Kelly: "Get over to the Four Reasons restaurant right away. There's a guy there trying to deduct a blonde from his income tax."

Kelly and Ira jump into their black limousine and with sirens wailing they drive through the streets of New York. They screech up to the restaurant where a crowd has gathered.

"Keep 'em back," Kelly says to a patrolman, who salutes.

As they try to enter, the manager rushes up to them. "This is the first time this has happened. We run a respectable place. This fellow came in with this blonde and he ordered two martinis. Then he ordered two more. Then he started nuzzling her. Then they ordered dinner—caviar, lobster thermidor, duck à l'orange, a Mouton Rothschild 1948, cherries jubilee, cognac, and coffee. They were holding hands and mushing it up, but we figured they were talking business.

"He called for the check. It came to $63.50. He signed it. Just as he was giving the waiter a tip, this other guy came in and took a pistol out of his pocket and fired six shots into the guy sitting with the dame. Then we figured maybe it wasn't a business dinner after all, so we called the Internal Revenue Service."

"That was good thinking," Ira says. "Did anyone touch anything?"

"Well, we had to clear the table. There were other customers waiting."

"Okay, we'll talk to the girl."

They go over to the blonde, who is crying on a bench.

"All right, sister, what happened?" Kelly asks.

"I refuse to answer any questions until I talk to my accountant," she says.

Ira says, "You better talk, miss. This is a very serious charge. Were you or were you not talking business during dinner?"

"Yes, we were, sort of. You see, I'm a buyer of drapes and he worked for the Aetna Curtain Company and he tried to sell me some curtains. He almost had me sold when he was—" She bursts into tears again.

"Who was the guy who shot him?"

"Sampson, of the Markay Curtain Company. He's been after my business also. He took me to lunch at the Colony and he thought we had an understanding."

"Was anything but business discussed tonight?"

"No, I swear it. We were going to go back to his apartment and sign the contract."

Ira says, "Okay, we'll take your word for it. But next time, no nuzzling. It gives the other taxpayers the wrong impression."

Kelly and Ira start to leave.

"But what about the murderer?" the manager asks.

Ira says, "He's innocent as far as we're concerned. Sampson can even deduct the gun, since he used it for a business purpose. But you did right to call us. You never can tell when some guy is trying to pad his expenses."

As they get back into their car they hear Mortimer Income's voice over the radio. "Car 54, get down to Pier 170 on the Hudson River. There is a yacht there loaded with show girls and the owner of it claims it's a company party. That is all."

The Old Soft Sell Being Sorely Taxed

IT'S GOING TO BE HARDER and harder to do business in the United States if the new income-tax regulations concerning expense accounts are carried out as promised by Commissioner Mortimer Caplin.

One of the most controversial items is that you can no longer entertain anyone for good-will purposes. You have to sell him either immediately before dinner, during dinner, or immediately after dinner.

You can't take out someone in hopes you'll get his business at some future date, nor can you entertain him if he has already given you his business. Under the regulations there will be no more soft sell. You either make a deal or you don't, on the spot, and you have to prove the deal was discussed or you can't write off the meal.

Not only will this cause hardship on businessmen, but I predict it will also break up friendships of long standing. No American likes to admit he's being entertained for a reason. Americans have been brought up to believe everyone loves them for themselves. It's going to be hard to admit that the only reason someone prized their company was because they were tax deductible.

I think the real problem is that the Internal Revenue people are ignorant of how American businessmen operate. When you're after somebody's business, there are certain formalities to be observed. It's too crude to invite someone to lunch and discuss what's really on your mind. The lunch or dinner is nothing more than a softening-up process. The one thing you should never discuss at it is the one thing you want to accomplish.

You discuss your golf game, you discuss your respective families, you discuss baseball, and you might even discuss your competitors, but American businessmen are too sophisticated to discuss business at a business lunch. This would let the cat out of the bag and spoil the whole meal.

Later on, perhaps during a phone conversation or a letter, you might indicate you could use the fellow's business, but he must feel that it's incidental to the warm friendship and high esteem in which you hold him as a fellow human being. He knows, and you know he knows, the lunch or dinner was part of the game, but there is an unwritten rule in business dealings that no one reminds the other he was entertained for any reason other than that he's your kind of a guy.

But now the Internal Revenue Service wants to make crass materialists of us all. They are saying in effect that we should no longer believe in the brotherhood of man. When we spend a buck we should make a buck, or pay for it out of our own pockets. They are forcing us to hold a gun against the ribs of our dinner guest, and tell him to put up or stop eating.

This isn't the American way of doing things. It is against

the principles of the National Association of Manufacturers, the United States Chamber of Commerce, and the Anti-Defamation League.

If the fathers of our Constitution wanted us to discuss business at business lunches they would have said so. Our country wouldn't be where it is today if John Jacob Astor, Jay Gould, Colonel Fisk, or Commodore Vanderbilt had to account for every cent they spent on entertainment.

Because of the new regulations this is how I'd have to account for my expenses in the future:

> Rented yacht for day on Potomac to see what was happening on the *Honey Fitz*, President Kennedy's yacht. He wasn't on board: $140.50.
>
> Went to Burning Tree golf course to play golf with brother-in-law who wanted to buy my old television set. Greens fees and yearly dues: $1,256.40. Deal consummated on seventeenth hole. Dinner and drinks to celebrate sale at Paul Young's restaurant: $30.56.
>
> Flew down to Miami to do column on troops at Key West. Stayed six days interviewing bartenders about troop morale: $456.60.
>
> Flew up to New York to see *Little Me*. Took father and sisters, as I hoped this good-will gesture would make it easier for me in my future business relations. Dinner at 21 restaurant and theater: $175.00.
>
> Went to Redskin football game with nine-year-old son, who said he had good idea for a column. Dinner afterward at Duke Zeibert's: $43.00.
>
> Bought new roof for house as I thought this would make a very funny column: $1,100.00.
>
> Had new grass put in as I wanted to do interview with landscape architect and this was the only way he would see me: $400.00.
>
> Entertained wife's friends from Dallas with cocktail and dinner party. Man from Dallas talked nothing but business: $340.00.
>
> Bought new drapes for living room for *McCall's* magazine piece: $600.00.
>
> Did a piece on color television as opposed to black and

white. Color television set: $550.00; black-and-white set: $350.00.

Enrolled son in private school so I could write funny article on Parent-Teacher Association. Tuition: $1,200.00.

Trip to Paris to cover opening of new Lido show: $1,550.00.

Wife suggested amusing column on buying French gowns. Bought gowns, but idea did not turn out as funny as expected. Gowns: $2,800.00.

Bought new oil burner, as I plan to do book on heating problems in the United States: $1,260.00.

New clothes for children so they can be photographed for piece I'm doing titled, "Why Johnny Can't Read": $180.00.

Taxi to Internal Revenue Service to protest items disallowed by unfriendly tax inspector: $1.50.

This will give you some idea of how difficult it will be in the future for someone to deduct legitimate expense items, and although there have been abuses by a few people, I don't see why the rest of us have to be penalized because of it.

Death and Taxes

A FEW MONTHS AGO, I devised a new tax plan which would change the whole system of taxation in the United States. I advocated that, instead of taxing the American people, we tax the American government, which has a lot more money than its citizens. I suggested the Government pay taxes on all the land it owns, on all the dams it runs, and all the letters it delivers. There would be a head tax on each member of the armed forces, and a speech tax on every member of Congress.

This plan was presented to Congress but no action was taken on it. So I am now presenting a new plan which I hope will get a better reception among our legislators and Treasury officials.

One of the reasons people don't like to pay taxes is they can't specify what their money should be spent for. All the money goes into one big bushel basket and is shoveled out by Government disbursing officers without a thought to the taxpayer's feelings. Under my plan every citizen could specify on his tax form what he wanted his money to be spent on. The money would be set aside for this purpose only, and couldn't be spent for anything else.

For example, suppose a taxpayer wanted to finance a junket to Europe for Congressman Adam Clayton Powell. He would write down that he wanted his taxes to go for this, and also specify how many secretaries Mr. Powell should take with him. On the other hand, a taxpaying doctor might ask that his contribution go for Medicare for the aged, and a steel executive might insist that his taxes only be spent on redecorating the White House. Southerners could specify that their money be spent to increase the salaries of the Supreme Court justices, and the members of the Teamsters Union might want to beef up the Attorney General's office.

It isn't necessary under the plan to stick to only one item. You could divvy up your taxes. You might specify five hundred dollars for a new highway to go through your town, one hundred dollars for Federal aid to education, fifty dollars for a new post office, one dollar for a Polaris submarine, and three cents for Chiang Kai-shek.

The important thing about this tax innovation is that it gives the people a say on how their taxes are to be spent. If nobody wants to give any money to Nasser, tough luck for Egypt. If people are fed up with farm surpluses, good-bye to price supports. If there are no contributions for germ warefare, then they have to let the germs go.

Right now everyone is probably interested in getting an American astronaut on the moon before the Russians. Under my new system the taxpayer could not only specify that he wants his tax money to go for this purpose, but he could also write in the name of the astronaut he wants to send. (It would be run along the same lines as the Miss Rheingold contest, and pictures of the astronauts would be posted on the walls of the Internal Revenue offices throughout the country.)

If Congress refused to authorize the money for a taxpayer's pet project, then the money would be returned to the taxpayer at the end of the fiscal year, plus 6 per cent interest. It's too bad my tax-reform bill isn't in effect this year as I would have been sure of a refund. I was going to request my money be spent exclusively on military aid for Cuba.

4.

MANAGING
THE NEWS

Management of News
Carries High Score

THE MANAGEMENT OF NEWS is still one of the main topics
of conversation in Washington. To tell the truth, it's very embarrassing for a newspaperman in Washington to admit no one
in Washington has tried to manage him; your status in the
town depends on who in the Government tried to manage you
and how.

This is how you rate in Washington from a news-manage-
ment point of view. If someone in the Administration has told
you a barefaced lie, you are credited with ten points. If he
has told you only part of the story, you get five points. If you
can name the person who gave you a news-managed story,
you are entitled to five points, but if you have to refer to him
as an "unimpeachable source" or a "high government official,"
you are entitled to only two points.

A "no comment" has no point value, but if Pierre Salinger
says he will neither "confirm nor deny" your story, you get
three points. By the same token if Pierre Salinger calls you up
and says the President didn't like the story you wrote, you get
twenty-five points. If Bobby Kennedy calls you up and says
he didn't like your story, you get thirty points. But if the President calls up himself and complains about something you've
written, you get fifty points and a round of free drinks at the
Press Club.

If Arthur Sylvester of the Defense Department declares a
story you wrote is pure "hogwash," you get ten points and a
plastic model of the new TFX, and if Secretary McNamara
says a story you wrote aided and abetted the enemy, you get
fifteen points and a free subscription to *Pravda*. If you can

prove Sylvester killed a story you wrote based on a Defense Department memo, you get five points, but you have to find a job for the person who gave you the memo. If you are not on speaking terms with anyone in the Administration because of something you wrote (two members of the White House staff must confirm this in writing), you get twenty points.

It's as easy to lose points as to get them under the present Administration. If, for example, a high official at the White House calls you up and congratulates you on what he considers was a "very fair" story, you lose your turn, you cannot pass "Go," and you cannot collect two hundred dollars. If a story is leaked to you as an Administration trial balloon and your colleagues find out about it, you lose your Press Club tie clasp and your dining privileges for a week.

During the Eisenhower Administration I had one of the highest point scores for managed news in the country. Because James Hagerty singled me out by name and said I wrote "unadulterated rot," I won the International News Management Trophy for 1958.

Unfortunately I started late in Washington this year and I have a score of only 134. I earned thirty-four points when I called Sylvester on the phone and he never returned my call. And I got one hundred points when President Kennedy canceled his subscription to the New York *Herald Tribune*.

Getting the News Is Always a Battle

THERE HAS BEEN a lot of talk about news management in the Government these days, but if you go through history you can find that every presidential administration tried to manage the press in one way or another. I found an old transcript the other day of a press briefing between Abraham Lincoln's press secretary and White House reporters, which shows that even in those days attempts were made to bottle up vital news of interest to the public.

Here are excerpts from it:

QUESTION: Mr. Nicolay, yesterday the President gave a speech at Gettysburg, and he started it out by saying, "Fourscore and seven years ago our fathers brought forth on this continent a new nation." Sir, would you mind telling us the names of the fathers he was referring to?

SECRETARY: I'm sorry, gentlemen. I can't reveal the names at this time.

QUESTION: The *Saturday Evening Post,* which is published in Philadelphia, said he was referring to Washington, Jefferson, and Franklin. Is that true?

SECRETARY: That's just conjecture. The President is not responsible for everything written by his friends.

QUESTION: The President said yesterday in the same speech that the country was engaged in a great civil war, testing whether that nation or any nation so conceived and so dedicated can long endure. He didn't say how he intended to win the war. Does this mean he has a no-win policy?

SECRETARY: The President in his speech was only concerned with the Battle of Gettysburg, which incidentally we won. The Department of War will give you full details on other battles.

QUESTION: The Department refuses to give us any information. We don't know how many troops were used at Gettysburg, who commanded them, or how many casualties there were. All we were given were some lousy photos of Confederate gun emplacements. How can we be sure the Confederates still don't have artillery hidden in the hills around Gettysburg?

SECRETARY: We have constant surveillance of the hills. To the best of our knowledge all Southern artillery pieces have been removed.

QUESTION: What about Confederate troops? There are an estimated seventeen thousand in the area.

SECRETARY: We have the South's promise they will be removed in due course.

QUESTION: Mr. Secretary, why didn't Mrs. Lincoln go with the President to Gettysburg?

SECRETARY: Mrs. Lincoln feels that her place is at home with her children. But she did send a telegram.

QUESTION: In talking about the government of the people, by the people, and for the people, did the President have any particular group in mind?

SECRETARY: Not to my knowledge, gentlemen. But I'll check it out just to make sure.

QUESTION: Mr. Secretary, didn't the President in his speech yesterday indicate he intended to manage the news?

SECRETARY: In what way?

QUESTION: He said, "The world will little note, nor long remember, what we say here." It seems to me in this phrase he was intimidating the newspapermen who were there.

SECRETARY: I don't think you have to interpret the speech in that manner. The President's remarks, written on an envelope, were off the cuff, and he felt there was no reason to be quoted. An official version of his speech will be made available to the press in due time, as soon as the President has a chance to go over it again.

Eyelash to Eyelash

THE UNITED STATES had a close scare when it was announced by Pamela Turnure, Mrs. Kennedy's press secretary, that a new policy would be instituted in regard to the coverage of the President's social events.

Covering White House social events has always been left to the women reporters, and in the first two years of the Kennedy Administration they were permitted to mingle with the guests, and even have a go at the buffet table. The most interesting tidbits to come out of the White House usually originated at a presidential reception, and the ladies of our pro-

fession depended on free access to the guests for the juicy items that graced the society pages the next day.

And so when Miss Turnure announced that under the new regulations there would be no more onsite inspections at diplomatic functions, and reporters could "watch" but not "mingle" with the guests, the reaction was one of dismay and anguish. To add insult to injury, Miss Turnure also informed them they would have to leave as soon as the President and Mrs. Kennedy arrived at the reception, and go home before the state reception really got swinging.

Well, you can imagine what went on in Washington when the new policy was announced. Society editors called their congressmen, Barry Goldwater canceled all leaves of his office staff, and four women reporters tried to commit hara-kiri with their Theta Sigma Phi sorority pins. For two days the women reporters and the White House staff were eyelash to eyelash and neither side would blink. A reception for the Washington diplomatic corps was scheduled for Thursday night and this was the test. If the "watch-but-not-mingle" order stayed in effect, the American people would be deprived of their main source of White House gossip.

Republican Representative Abner W. Sibal of Connecticut was horrified when he heard about the new policy, and said, "The Kennedys are not the owners of the White House. They just have a four-year lease. The American people own it and are interested in who is being wined and dined there by the First Family." He also said the Kennedy family was trying to make the White House into another Buckingham Palace.

Well, fortunately for everyone, on the night of the diplomatic reception, Mrs. Kennedy blinked, and the White House order was rescinded. The reporters covering the event were not only allowed to mingle with the guests, but were also urged to sample the cold cuts on the buffet table.

It was a close call for all concerned, and it does raise a point for the future. How much right does the public have to know what is going on socially at the residence of the President and the First Lady?

I have always taken the position the Kennedys should have no secrets from the American public, as long as they live in the White House. I believe Representative Sibal didn't go far enough in his statement. It is my opinion that there should be a constant flow of social news out of the White House at all times.

There are still functions at the White House from which reporters are excluded. For example, when the President and Mrs. Kennedy have breakfast together in the morning, the press is forbidden to attend. Why? What do they have to say to each other at breakfast that the American public couldn't hear?

Sometimes it's rumored that the President plays with his children without a single reporter in the room. We didn't elect a man so he could turn into a recluse!

Election Coverage Computed

I WAS VERY IMPRESSED with the television coverage of the last elections. Not only was I treated to up-to-the-minute results of the contests, but each network tried to outdo itself in giving me an analysis of the returns and what they meant long before the final figures were in.

Every network had its own computer working for it and, by feeding the early results into the machine, gave us all a preview of what would surely happen later on. Here is how it seemed to go, at least to me.

". . . And now let's see what is happening in the Midwest. Chuck, do you have anything to report?"

"Yes, Chet, something very interesting is happening here in the State of Congestion. The incumbent Governor Gruengruen is leading his opponent Ezekial Habit by 5,489,430 to 30. Now ordinarily this would make Governor Gruengruen the winner, but our computer shows that in 1946 Governor Gruengruen was leading by six million votes to twenty-five but lost out when two rural counties from upstate went for his opponent Long John Johns. So on the basis of the returns so far I would say Ezekial Habit will probably squeak through and get a one per cent majority, which of course will be an upset."

I switched channels and got Walter, who was saying, "Do you have any news for us from the Far West, Sidney?"

"Yes, Walter, I do. The Western picture looks cloudy at this moment and it's Touch and Go. Congressman Sam Touch has been fighting State Assemblyman Go in a very interesting race. Touch received 158,002 votes, and Go 158,001 votes, but we are still waiting for the Rocky Mountain districts to report. Touch is very strong in the mountains as he goes skiing there every winter. We must keep in mind, however, Go goes fishing there in the summer, and at this stage it could be anybody's race."

"What does the computer say, Sidney?"

"Every time I ask it, it replies: 'Do you mind if I do the results from the East first?'"

"Well, we'll get back to you, Sidney. Now let's get an analysis on the over-all picture from Henry. How does it look to you, Henry?"

"There are some very exciting trends here, Walter. So far the computer has conceded the defeat of five Governors and four Senators in spite of the fact that the Governors and Senators refuse to concede themselves. Now I've just telephoned the candidates and asked them to concede gracefully to the computers, but they refuse to give up. For example, Governor Wrinkles is winning in Fall State by one million votes, yet the computer tells us these votes do not mean anything. "Wrinkles is still holding on, though the election, according to the computer, will be won by his opponent, Coroner William Casey."

I turned to another channel and heard someone say, "Dave, I've just talked to the State of Agitation and there is a lot of excitement up there because Governor Gluckstern has just announced now that the returns are in he's going to divorce Mrs. Gluckstern. This is the fourth time Governor Gluckstern has been divorced. It is also the fourth time he will serve as Governor. The computer predicted Governor Gluckstern's victory and also his divorce, but it hasn't predicted how much alimony he will have to pay. We'll have those figures for you in a moment."

More Than Starlings

THE WHITE HOUSE has taken off against starlings and well it should. For years various Presidents of the United States have been bothered by these pests which roost on the beautiful façade and in the trees, making a mess of the President's carefully worked-out programs.

Now, according to a White House spokesman, a recording of a distressed starling is being played in the trees, and it is hoped that when other starlings hear it they will be frightened away. The White House even played the record of the distressed starling for unbelieving newspapermen. The spokesman was then asked why the starling on the record was in distress. The spokesman replied he did not know, but there was no need to hurt a starling to make it cry out. At this point a man from the *National Geographic Magazine* revealed that the way to make a starling scream out in distress was to hang it upside down by its feet.

This is all well and good for starlings, but they haven't been the Administration's only problem. Lately the New Frontier has been bothered by news leaks in the Pentagon and the State Department, so much so that directives have come out warning State and Defense Departments' personnel against talking to newspapermen without reporting it to their respective press officers.

In the case of the Defense Department, Assistant Secretary of Defense Arthur Sylvester has instituted a monitor system, where no one may talk to a member of the press without sending Sylvester a memo or having a third person, from his office, present. This, of course, is all in the interest of national security, though there are some skeptics who claim it could also be used to cover up a lot of blunders. But what Mr. Sylvester could do if he was really determined to keep the press away from the Pentagon is, instead of playing a recording of a distressed starling, to set up a loudspeaker outside the Pentagon and play a record of a screaming, distressed journalist, thus scaring other journalists away from the building.

Now the question is: how do you distress a journalist? Quite simple. You refuse to tell him the truth, and immediately he's in great pain and yelling at the top of his voice.

What Mr. Sylvester might do at his next press briefing is to record the voices of several newspapermen as he tells them he has no intention of answering their questions. If the quality of the record isn't good enough, Mr. Sylvester can always hang one of the newspapermen upside down while issuing his famous "It's none of your business" comment.

Of course, it's quite possible that this method of keeping reporters away might not succeed and they will be attracted by the screams instead of repelled. If this is the case, then I think the Administration will have to get tougher with the press just as you have to get tougher with starlings. They might have to electify the outside of the Pentagon and State Department buildings. In case a newspaperman tries to get in, he will be given a real shock.

This may sound a little cruel, but we're living in desperate times. So the only solution is to scare the press away from our public buildings before they make a bigger mess than the starlings.

Best Stories of 1962

EVERY YEAR I pick the best news stories of the year. Many of them have never been reported before; others have been lost among the classified and real-estate ads.

The first has to do with a stamp collector named Jonathan

Kincaid, who used to buy sheets of newly issued stamps as
soon as they were put on sale by the United States Post Office.

Mr. Kincaid, who made eighty dollars a week as a contact
man for a contact-lens company, went down to the post office
one day and bought a sheet of a new stamp that was honoring
the aborted Bay of Pigs landing in Cuba. But when Kincaid
got home he noticed there were American airplanes printed
on the stamp, and since there were no airplanes at the Bay
of Pigs, Kincaid realized that someone in the printing office
had made a grave error.

He called up the newspapers and told them that he had a
sheet of misprinted stamps that were worth $200,000. The
newspapers immediately called Postmaster General J. Edward
Day and informed him of the printing error. They asked him
what he intended to do about it.

Mr. Day was adamant. "When the United States Post Office
makes a mistake, we should pay for it. We shall give Mr.
Kincaid the $200,000 he is asking, and we will pay anybody
else $200,000 for a similar misprinted sheet. To do otherwise
would make a mockery of stamp collecting throughout the
world."

The second story has to do with Abraham Lincoln Roosevelt, a Negro student who wanted to enroll at the University
of Mississippi.

Mr. Roosevelt, a straight "A" student in high school, made
his application to the admissions office, and was immediately
accepted by the University. On his first day of school he was
asked to join a fraternity, and several students invited him to
the freshman prom. He was elected class president and cheer-
leader and a member of the exclusive Knife and Fork Club.
In a couple of weeks Mr. Roosevelt was editing the college
humor magazine, was active in the dramatic society, chairman
of the blood bank, member of the Student Council, manager
of the football team, and captain of the debating squad.

By the end of the first term, Mr. Roosevelt flunked all his
courses and was thrown out of the school.

"They made me do so many extracurricular activities," Mr.

Roosevelt said bitterly, "I didn't have time to do any studying."

Major Carl Lemuel was selected as one of the original United States astronauts to go into space. Major Lemuel went through all the training and it was his turn to go up next. But a week before he was to be shot into space the doctors discovered he had a bad kidney, and said he couldn't possibly go into orbit.

In an interview after the medical examination Major Lemuel said, "I couldn't be happier. I was wondering how I was going to get out of it. I think anyone who goes up in one of those capsules is nuts, and it doesn't prove anything anyway."

Edward Kennedy, a thirty-year-old citizen of Massachusetts, decided to run for United States Senator on the Democratic ticket. A group of citizens came to him and said, "Teddy, your brother is President of the United States, your other brother is Attorney General, your brother-in-law is head of the Peace Corps. It will look awfully bad if there is another Kennedy in Washington. Why don't you give up the idea of running for Senator so that you don't embarrass the Party?"

"But what else can I do?" Mr. Kennedy asked.

The citizens thought and thought, but no one could come up with an answer.

That's My Boy

"So how come," Aunt Molly asked my father the other day at a family reunion, "if Arthur's stationed in Washington we never see him on television at the President's press conference?"

"Maybe," said Cousin Milton maliciously, "he isn't allowed to attend the President's press conference. They're not just open to everybody."

Uncle Oscar said, "It's getting very embarrassing. The day

after a Kennedy press conference all my friends say to me, 'So where was your big-shot nephew that you're always talking about?' I'm telling you, it's no fun going to work any more."

Uncle Leo said, "Let's face it. A Joseph Alsop he's not."

It was more than Pop could take and he called me up the next day. "The whole family's disgusted with you," he said. "You've been in Washington six months and they haven't seen you once on a Kennedy press conference."

"Pop," I said, "it's very hard to get on television at a presidential press conference. The only way to do it is to ask a question."

"So ask a question," he said. "It's going to kill you?"

"I never know what to ask the President," I told him.

"Why don't you ask him if he's willing to take a lie-detector test?"

"Pop, I can't ask him that. Besides, even if I thought of a good question to ask, the President still might not call on me. You see, you have to jump up at a press conference and then the President recognizes you. Sometimes you can jump up and down for thirty minutes and nothing happens. Then you have to have a long question so the cameras can focus on you. Before television the questions were very short. But now, in most cases, the questions are longer than the President's answers. It's hard for me to think up a long question."

"Enough excuses," Pop said. "All I know is the family is getting sick and tired of looking for you on TV. You better do something about it because I can't keep thinking up excuses for you."

Pop hung up and I started to stew. It was true, I had let the family down, but I didn't know what to do about it. So I took my problem to Ken Crawford, columnist of *Newsweek* magazine.

"Don't worry," he said. "I had the same problem too. Family wouldn't talk to me for months, but then I solved it."

"How?" I asked.

"Every time I go to a press conference, I sit behind someone who is sure to ask a question. In that way when the camera is on him or her, it's also on me. Come on, I'll take you over to the press conference and you can see for yourself."

I went over with him. "There," he said, "We'll sit behind May Craig of the Portland *Press*. She's sure to ask a question."

We grabbed two seats behind May Craig, who was wearing a nice pink hat.

"Just wait," Mr. Crawford said. "But be ready at any time."

The President's press conference started. Miss Craig jumped up and down as if she were on a puppet string, and, sure enough, the President called on her to ask question number 6, which was: "Mr. President, two weeks ago six Republican members of the Joint Economic Committee—House and Senate—wrote you a long letter of suggestions about Federal expenditures including a request that you establish a presidential commission on Federal expenditures similar to the Clay Commission on Foreign Aid. What would be your position on that suggestion?"

For thirty seconds, as Miss Craig asked her question, I scratched my ear, waved my hand discreetly, and stared into the camera, grinning.

That night I got a call from Pop. "Well," he said happily, "the whole family is talking about you. I'm proud of you, son. I knew you'd come through."

"Don't mention it, Pop. It was just a matter of time."

"There's one thing, though," Pop said. "We all felt that friend of yours, Ken Crawford, was hogging the camera."

5.

INSTANT
CULTURE

Anything Can Happen

THE WASHINGTON GALLERY OF MODERN ART is holding a "Pop Art Festival." Pop art, in case you're wondering, is the latest thing, in which artists use anything from comic strips to American flags to give a new concept to reality and illusion. (It's more than that too, but I'm not sure how much more.)

In conjunction with the festival the Washington Gallery is holding two Happenings, under the direction of Claes Oldenburg. Mr. Oldenburg has held Happenings all over the country and he was brought to Washinton at great expense to hold them here.

I had lunch with Mr. Oldenburg, Mrs. Alice M. Denney, assistant director of the gallery, and Mrs. John Mecklin, who is doing publicity for the Happenings.

"Mr. Oldenburg," I said, "what is a Happening?"

"There is no definition. I don't know myself what a Happening is. It's putting all the elements and senses together and composing a picture. Sight, sound, smell, imagination. Everything plays a part."

"I see," I said. "How do you organize a Happening?"

"I buy things at the Goodwill Industries, the Salvation Army, and secondhand shops. Then I find a place to have a Happening in. It must have three-dimensional space, and it's best if the thing you find is characteristic of the composition you're trying to create."

"Naturally," I said. "Where is your Happening going to take place?"

"I've had a lot of difficulty finding the right spot. You see, at a Happening the place where you do it is as important as what you do. I found a rug-cleaning shop which looked just perfect, since there was lots of junk in it. But the fire department wouldn't let me use it. Fire departments and police departments and vice squads give us the most trouble about our Happenings."

"That's because they're square," I said.

"So I've decided to give my Happening in the Washington Gallery itself. Now I know you're going to say this violates the idea of holding a Happening in a typical place. But in this case the gallery is okay because the walls are white and it's typical of the Washingtonian's yearning for everything in the city to be white. Therefore it's really a good place for a Happening."

"All right," I said, "so you have the place for the Happening. Now what happens?"

"I'm not sure," Mr. Oldenburg said. "I have to find things for the Happening and people to play parts in it. But don't get me wrong. I don't hold a Happening with any preconceptions. I use what I experience myself. For example, they have had three fires in the hotel where I'm staying."

"You're not going to set the gallery on fire, are you?" Mrs. Denney asked in alarm.

"No," said Mr. Oldenburg, "though it is an interesting thought."

"Maybe you could just have a smoldering mattress," I suggested.

"The fire department wouldn't allow it," he said.

"What do people do at a Happening?"

"It's hard to say," Mr. Oldenburg said. "They usually stand up, though I have seated them at times. Once I had a girl walking up and down a corridor saluting, and once I had a fellow break up a table with a rubber mallet. I was interested only in the repetition of the hammering—the climax of the table's being broken had no significance."

"I can see that," I said. "Has anything ever happened at a Happening you know of?"

"Once we built an eighteen-foot airplane of muslin and dropped it on the audience. I guess you could say something happened. But I'm not concerned with whether a Happening

is a success or not. The fact that it happened is all I care about."

As we left the restaurant we stopped by Mrs. Denney's station wagon, which she had lent Mr. Oldenburg to scout for things for the Happening. In the back were a baby carriage, six small footstools, a bird cage, a first baseman's mitt, a mirror, an iron bedstead, and two pairs of saddle shoes.

"What are you going to do with all that?" I asked.

"I don't know," Mr. Oldenburg said. "I might use them in the Happening and I might not. It all depends on how I feel."

Machines Take Over

PEOPLE DON'T REALIZE IT, but it won't be very long before teaching machines are perfected to the point where it won't be necessary to have teachers at all. The teaching-machine industry is working night and day to perfect new machines which will not only help make up for the teacher shortage in the United States but will also cut down on the cost of hiring new teachers. It is not too far-fetched to predict that in ten or twenty years our children will be sitting in teacherless classes, their work programmed for them by computers, graded by IBM cards, and scolded for sloppy work by closed-television monitors fifty miles away.

While there are great advantages to learning by machine, we should never lose sight of the human element. It is for this reason that we have perfected the Robot Teaching Machine, which will combine all the advantages of machine learning with those of being taught by a teacher in the room. The Robot Teaching Machine would work as follows: each seat would be magnetized, and there would be a small piece of metal sewn into the seat of each student's clothes. When the class was in session, the student would not be able to get out of his seat.

If a child had to go to the bathroom, he would push a

button on his desk. The computer in front of the room would then break the field of magnetism and allow the child to go to the bathroom, providing there was only one pupil out of the room at a time.

If a child misbehaved in class, the computer would send out a slight shock which would be the equivalent of a rapped knuckle. If the child still refused to behave and the shock treatment were not punishment enough, he would be lifted out of his seat by a conveyor belt and carried to the principal's office. There the principal computer would deal with the pupil. When the pupil arrived at the principal computer's office, the machine would automatically sound an alarm in the home of the pupil's parents and one of them would have to come to school and discuss his child with the computer. The principal computer would have stored in it several lectures on tape, and would play the one most suitable for the occasion.

The Robot Teaching Machine would be as humane as possible. If a little boy or little girl started to cry in class, the machine would start dispensing facial tissue. If the child continued to cry, there would be a portable lap on the side of the machine where the child could find comfort.

During lunch periods the computer would turn into a vending machine where the student could buy milk, sandwiches, hot soup, and candy bars. The profits from these would go into buying athletic machines for recreational purposes.

Now, someone is going to raise the question of how you can prevent cheating on tests without a teacher in the room. Quite simple. Before each child hands in his IBM paper, he will attach a blood-pressure valve to his arm and take a lie-detector test. If the graph shows he cheated, he gets three shocks and has to take the test over again.

The object of the machine is to make the child love and respect it. Some machines will be better than others. If a machine breaks down, a substitute machine will teach for the day.

Some children may want to show their affection for a teaching computer. Instead of bringing the machine an apple or flowers, the child could bring it a can of oil or a new transistor.

What's Wrong with TV

I WAS TALKING the other day with "My Son, the Folk Singer," Allan Sherman, and we got around to the question of what was wrong with television. We both came to the conclusion that everyone on TV was being presented in a false light, and the public was being cheated out of seeing situations as they really are. For example, on the lawyer shows *Perry Mason* and *The Defenders,* no one ever asks for a fee. There is never any discussion of money on these programs and people are under the impression that any lawyer will defend you for the love of it.

But in real life this is what would happen. A woman comes into Perry Mason's office. She says, "My son has been accused of a crime, but I know he didn't do it."

Perry in real life would say, "Wait a minute, madam. Before you go any further, I'll have to ask for a retainer."

"He's innocent," the lady says. "You've got to defend him."

"How much can you afford? Legal costs are expensive. If he pleads guilty, I'll make a deal with the District Attorney and save you the expense of a long drawn-out jury trial."

"But he wants to plead not guilty."

"Big deal," says Perry. "They'll probably hang him anyway and it will still cost you five thousand dollars."

"I guess you're right," the woman says. "Plead him guilty. He's always getting into trouble, anyway."

"That will be five hundred dollars now and five hundred more at the start of the trial. If there are any other expenses, I'll let you know."

Or let's take Dr. Kildare. What kind of guy would Dr.

Kildare be if he weren't on television? Perhaps something like this.

"Dr. Kildare," an elderly man says, "I have a pain in my side."

"I don't know anything about pains in people's sides. I'll send you to a specialist, Dr. Renfrow."

"But besides my side, my left leg hurts."

"Why didn't you say so in the first place? Dr. Martin is the best leg man in town. Tell him I sent you."

"And it hurts when I breathe."

"You need a good lung man. After you see Dr. Martin about your leg, go over and see Dr. Steele about your chest. I'll write down the address here."

"I can't read your handwriting," the old man says.

"Eye trouble, too? You better see Dr. Rabb, the eye, ear, nose, and throat man."

"Thank you very much, Dr. Kildare."

"Don't mention it. That will be ten dollars."

What about Dr. Ben Casey, if there were such a person in real life?

A nurse rushes in. "Dr. Casey, there's been a terrible skiing accident. They want you in the operating room right away."

Casey puts on a mask, sterilizes his arms, walks over to the table.

"Has this man signed a release that I'm not responsible if the operation doesn't come off?"

"No, sir. He was brought in unconscious."

"Well, I'm not operating until someone signs a release. Do you think I'm going to be sued for malpractice?"

"But, doctor, if you don't operate at once, he'll die."

"And if he dies," Dr. Casey says, "the next of kin will blame me. No, thank you. No release, no operation. My lawyer won't let me do it any other way."

The final thing to make one suspect television of not being true to life is that taxis are always plentiful on TV and ready to pursue the heavy.

This is what would happen in real life if a private eye like Peter Gunn tried to follow someone.

"Taxi, taxi! Follow that cab!"

"Waddaya mean follow that cab?"

"I want you to follow that cab, like I said."

"Look, mister, I pick people up and take them to a destination. I don't follow no cabs."

"You're letting him get away."

"Get yourself another hack. I got a wife and kid to think of, and I don't have time to get involved in any cops-and-robbers stuff."

"You mean you refuse to follow that cab?"

"Out, mister, you've been watching too many television shows."

Pierre Writes to François

MY CHER FRANÇOIS,

Under separate cover we are sending you the *Mona Lisa*.

Since you are the only Frenchman I know living in America, I am begging you to look after our dear beloved *La Joconde*. You cannot believe the consternation and bitterness that there is in France because she has been shipped off to the United States to be ogled by millions of uncultured and ignorant Americans.

The French still don't know what happened that she should have been allowed to leave the country, but they suspect it it had to do with a secret deal between de Gaulle and President Kennedy. Gaston, who is up on these matters, says he has it on highest authority that de Gaulle agreed to send the *Mona Lisa* to the United States if Kennedy would drop the Skybolt missile program, thus embarrassing Britain and making her join the Common Market on France's terms.

Phillippe is certain it had something to do with Cuba. He says a deal had been made that if the Russians moved their missiles out of Cuba, the French would move the *Mona Lisa* out of the Louvre. He said he read it in the *Saturday Evening Post*.

As for my own theory, I think a woman was behind it. I think what happened was that Mrs. Kennedy said to Malraux when he was in Washington, "I wonder how the *Mona Lisa* would look in the Blue Room," and our Cultural Minister said, "Why don't I send it over so you can see for yourself?"

What our cabinet members won't do these days for a beautiful woman who speaks French!

Last night I went to the Café Flore for an *apéritif* and a battle was raging in the café over *Mona's* absence.

An Italian student said *La Joconde* didn't belong to us in the first place and should be in Florence, so he was thrown out in front of a bus on the Boulevard St. Germain des Prés. Free speech is one thing, but saying *La Joconde* does not belong to us is incitement to riot.

Jean-Paul asked the question that was on everybody's mind, which was, "How do we know we're going to get it back?" And Ponto said, "Yes, and if we do get it back, how do we know what condition it will be in?" Alain summed it up for all of us when he said, "And even if we know what condition it will be in, how do we know that is the condition we want it to be in?"

A precedent has been set, François, and we don't intend to take this loan lightly. We are going to get our revenge. The next time Arthur Schlesinger comes to France we're going to ask Mrs. de Gaulle to ask him if he would let the Louvre borrow the Lincoln Memorial for a few months. He will have to say yes, and then let's see how the Americans feel.

You as a Frenchman, François, can appreciate the anguish that we are going through here with our beautiful mistress flitting about between Washington and New York where everyone knows the temperature is not fit for a lady of her complexion.

But I am sure the Americans do not know how we feel. I think the only way to explain it to them is to ask them what reaction they would have if someone crated up their Jacqueline Kennedy in an air-conditioned plastic box, placed her on the SS *United States,* and shipped her off to Paris for four months.

Take care of our little girl.

Your cher ami,
Pierre

First Official Function

MY FIRST OFFICIAL Washington function is something I'll remember for the rest of my life. It was the black-tie, long-evening-dress opening of the *Mona Lisa* at the National Gallery, and my wife couldn't have been more excited if she had been invited to go water-skiing with John Glenn at Hyannis Port.

When the invitation arrived she couldn't believe it. She was waiting for me when I came home from the office and she threw her arms around me. "We've been invited to something," she cried. "And after only four months in Washington. It's hard to believe."

"What have we been invited to?"

"The unveiling of the *Mona Lisa* and the invitation says the President is going to be there and André Malraux and probably all of the Cabinet and the Supreme Court and the diplomatic corps and the members of Congress and everything. Isn't it exciting?"

I held her close. "Our first Washington function. I wonder if we're up to it."

"I'll have to buy a new dress," she said.

"Spend, spend," I chortled. "These things don't happen every day."

"And I'll need new shoes and gloves, and I'll have to have my hair changed and my nails done. I just don't know where to start."

"Just don't look more beautiful than Jackie," I chided. "I guess it wouldn't hurt to buy a new tuxedo. This will probably be the first of many White House functions. After all, once they put you on the list, they can hardly take you off."

"I have to call my mother," my wife said. "And my sister Pat, and my sister Joanie, and my sister Sue."

"Call, call. That is what long distance is for."

For the next two weeks we could talk of nothing else. Would the President speak to us? Would Malraux ask us to say a few words about the *Mona Lisa?* Would Vice-President Johnson insist on introducing us to his wife?

My wife read every protocol manual she could get her hands on. "It doesn't say anything in any of them about what to do at the unveiling of a painting," she said.

"Just be yourself," I told her. "The Kennedys are not particular about protocol."

The big night finally came. My wife had spent five hundred dollars on a dress, thirty dollars at the hairdresser's, one hundred dollars for accessories. But she could hardly have spent less for such an important social engagement. Paul Young, the restaurateur, lent me his Rolls-Royce so we could arrive in style. My new tuxedo was cut straight from the cloth of the New Frontier.

At the door of the National Gallery, United States Marines stood at attention under a long canvas archway. It was all I had dreamed it would be. I squeezed my wife's hand as we entered the building.

After checking our coats, we rode up in the elevator to the second floor with two admirals, three Senators, and four ambassadors, and their wives. Both of us were starry-eyed. Then we stepped out of the elevator into the beautiful rotunda.

We couldn't see anything except a mob of people standing facing a bunch of arc lights way off in the distance. We stood patiently in the crowd staring at the lights. Obviously they were going to let the crowd in all at once. A half-hour passed. We were now hemmed in from behind. Another half-hour passed. Nothing happened.

We heard some static over a loudspeaker and some applause. The arc lights were blinding us. Another half-hour passed. Nobody moved. Bodies were pressed tightly together. Ambassadors perspired, congressmen muttered. More static, then more applause, and then suddenly everyone turned around.

"That's it," said someone.

"What's it?" I asked.

"It's all over."

"What happened?" I asked him.

"How the hell do I know?"

"What do we do now?"

"You go home."

"Where's the President?"

"He went home too."

"But we haven't even seen the *Mona Lisa*."

"You can see it on television tomorrow morning at 8:30."

My wife was heartbroken and was crying in the cloakroom. An old experienced Washington hand tried to comfort her.

"It's all right, dear," the lady said. "You'll get over it. The first function is always the worst. After a while you get used to it. What a pretty dress you're wearing."

This last remark made my wife cry even more.

The Smile of Mona Lisa

WHEN THE MONA LISA, the Louvre's own pride and joy, came to Washington, everyone was thrilled with the news. As an old Paris hand, I've had more than a nodding acquaintance with *"La Joconde,"* as we Montparnasse types used to call her.

As a matter of fact, it was only about six years ago that a group of us sitting at a table at the Café Dôme got into a discussion about the masterpiece. The question we were discussing was, "Why was the *Mona Lisa* smiling?" Pretty soon the entire café was involved in the debate, and it raged, as

all discussions of this type did, until the early hours of the morning.

It was agreed by almost everybody that she was smiling over something Leonardo da Vinci had said. But what? Obviously it wasn't a joke or she would have been laughing.

"Perhaps," one of my friends suggested, "he said to her, 'I just do these portraits to earn some extra money. I'm really an abstract painter at heart.'"

"No, I think he probably said, 'I'll admit Michelangelo has an interesting technique, but you really can't call him a serious painter.'"

"What about him saying, 'Don't talk to me about Michelangelo. Any guy who paints ceilings for a living has really sold out.'"

A young lady in the group disagreed. "I think he said, 'It may be amusing to you, but try painting with a broken arm sometime and see how far you get.'"

"I know," a former GI chimed in. "Da Vinci had just said to her, 'And as soon as we get this finished for *Good Housekeeping,* we'll do one for *Playboy.*'"

"Perhaps they weren't talking about art at all," a writer said. "Perhaps da Vinci was telling her about some of his inventions. Suppose he said to her, 'And then I'll put wings on it and I'll call it an airplane.'"

"No, no, no!" came from a table across the room. "He said to her, 'How come you get your dishes so clean and yet keep your hands so smooth?'"

Another student said, "We're overlooking the obvious. Leonardo said to her at that moment, 'Have you ever thought of serving spaghetti with sea food instead of meat balls?'"

A Left Bank lover was adamant. "Your theories are all cockeyed. What he said to her was, 'Well, if you weren't married, would you consider going away with me to Venice for the weekend?'"

The café shouted him down. "Keep sex out of it."

Students on the Left Bank in those days were easily shocked.

"Could he have said, 'And the correspondence school ad said if I send in this picture with twenty-five florins I might win ten free art lessons by mail'?"

"You're all wrong," the waiter said. "It is a matter of record that da Vinci said only two words to La Joconde when he painted her."

"What were they?"

" 'You're what?' "

Save Lincoln Center!

THE WAY THEY BUILD and tear down buildings in New York City, I've decided it's not too early to start a Save Lincoln Center Committee. I know this venerable hall is almost a year old, but there is still a lot of life left in her, and as Chairman of the Committee, I think it would be a mistake to demolish the building in favor of a parking lot, a Hilton Hotel, or a new Pennsylvania Station. Sure, you say, we've got to make way for progress, but there are still some traditions left in New York, and the Lincoln Center Philharmonic Hall is one of them.

The Lincoln Center is a world-wide symbol of culture. It's true people have sat in the seats and musicians have sat on the stage, but is that any reason to tear it down? Just because a building has been used *once* is no reason to decide it's served its function and that we must now make way for something new.

For those of us who have been closely connected with Lincoln Center during the past year, I can only remind others of the hallowed memories this historical building holds for all of us. It seems like only yesterday I watched Leonard Bernstein conduct the New York Philharmonic Orchestra while our First Lady watched with approval from the presidential box. Time has passed since then and the great names of the music world have performed there—Van Cliburn, Richard Tucker, Jennie Tourel, Eileen Farrell, George London, Eugene

Ormandy, and Adlai Stevenson. And still, just because of its age, people want to raze it.

Plans are now underway by the Committee to hold a rally at Carnegie Hall to *Save Lincoln Center.*

The Committee is going to ask everyone who was at Lincoln Center on opening night to show up in formal clothes to protest with placards and petitions. The police and firemen's band will play for the benefit, and the money raised will go not only to carry on the fight, but also to redecorate the hall and refurbish the seats.

A Save Lincoln Center ball is now in the works and Lawrence Welk will conduct the hit show tunes of Leonard Bernstein. My wife, who is in charge of the Women's Auxiliary, has already scheduled three teas to raise funds for a new façade which will bring the outside of the building up to date with the rest of the architecture in the neighborhood.

Acoustically speaking, the Lincoln Center's Philharmonic Hall is still excellent and the passage of time has only improved the wonderful sounds that emanate from the rafters. If you had to duplicate the acoustics for a new hall, it would cost at least two million dollars.

Unfortunately, as soon as it was announced that a Save Lincoln Center Committee had been formed, a counterorganization was started which wants to move Lincoln Center to Las Vegas, the cultural capital of the United States. Las Vegas feels that if it had had the Lincoln Center, it would have gotten the Floyd Patterson–Sonny Liston fight.

The battle has just started and we need everyone's support. It's not too late to write to your congressman and Senator. Send telegrams to Governor Rockefeller and Mayor Wagner. Call up one of the Kennedys. There is still time to beat the demolition teams if you *act now.*

A lot of people may say I'm unnecessarily worried, and that Lincoln Center may still be with us next year. That may be so, but on opening night I saw William Zeckendorf and his son in front of the hall with surveying tools, and everybody in New York knows what that means.

Anyone for Acoustics?

EVER SINCE the Lincoln Center Philharmonic Hall opened there has been a lot of talk about acoustics. America has suddenly become acoustics-conscious and it's a wonderful thing to see.

I was hoping to interview the acoustics engineer at Lincoln Center, but unfortunately he was not available on opening night. So I had to settle for another acoustics expert, Mr. Sam Reverberation, who is famous for doing the acoustics at the Yankee Stadium and the Forty-second Street station of the Eighth Avenue subway.

I caught Mr. Reverberation during intermission at the Philharmonic Hall, and, while he had nothing to do with the acoustics at the hall, he was perfectly willing to talk about them.

"Sir," I said, "I would like to get your opinion of the acoustics at this wonderful hall."

He cupped his ear and said, "Eh?"

"I SAID I WOULD LIKE TO GET YOUR OPINION OF THE ACOUSTICS."

"Acrostics. I don't do acrostics, young fellow. I guess I should. It would take my mind off acoustics."

"Mr. Reverberation, do you think using hexagonal gold clouds in a hall is a sound practice?"

"Yup, I once used a round mattress. Absorbed everything. Unfortunately it didn't look so good hanging from the ceiling."

"There is a rumor, sir, that there is a deficiency in the cello tone."

"Yes, that's good. Many of us engineers use Jello as a material. It wiggles a little, but it does keep out the sound, and the colors *are* nice."

"They also said there were some dead spots in the hall."

"What a shame," he said. "I'm sorry about that, but we all have to go sometime."

"Sir, how do you feel about the sound from the rostrum."

"No, sir, we rarely do a rest-room. We're only concerned with the hall itself. That's where they want to spend the money. We will do a rest-room if they ask us, but we have to charge extra."

"Do you feel that there is an echo in the hall?"

"Just say it once, young feller. I heard you the first time."

"What about the criticism that there is a definite lack of bass?"

"Yup, we always lacquer the base. It gives the hall a nice Oriental effect."

"Can wrong acoustics cause aggravated hearing?" I asked him.

"What in the devil does marinated herring have to do with what we're talking about? Are you sure you're a newspaperman?"

"No, sir. That isn't what I mean."

"Oh, sure, you meet a lot of mean newspapermen in this business. But you meet some nice ones, too."

"Based on the experience of halls such as this, do you have any advice for hi-fi bugs?"

"No sir. Termite control takes care of the bugs. We don't even start our work until they're finished."

"To be a sound engineer, do you have to have a special background?"

"Yes, but you can also use Fiberglas and wool."

"Just one more question, sir. The horn is sounding for me to return to my seat."

He looked at me and said, "What horn?"

"This is the question, sir. Do you approve of lowering the panels by motorized winch?"

"That story was a complete lie," he said indignantly. "She was a nice girl and besides she was walking."

A New Status Symbol

THERE'S A NEW STATUS SYMBOL for the American woman, and if it catches on a lot of professional writers are going to be in trouble. It has not been uncommon in the past to hear a woman say, "My life would make a wonderful book if it could only be put down on paper."

It's usually ended there, but recently, if I am to believe Mr. S. J. Michelson, who runs a ghost-writing service in New York, the more well-heeled women are finally starting to do something about it. They're hiring ghost writers to write their books, and paying publishers to print them.

There is nothing like having your own book between hard covers to impress the neighborhood. For prestige it beats a mink coat, a foreign car, and a trip to Europe, and thanks to people like Mr. Michelson, anyone can write a book now—if she has the money.

Every housewife with a literary bent dreams of writing another *Peyton Place,* which will not only bring her fame and wealth but will also take care of all the people in her town that she holds a grudge against.

Not only does a published book give a woman social esteem but it gives her an outlet for her frustrations and emotions, and Mr. Michelson, who works with a tape recorder, figures it costs just as much to write a book and get everything out of your system, as it does to see a psychiatrist. And at the end of the treatment you have something to show for your investment. Mr. Michelson says all he needs with a woman is about two or three sessions with a tape recorder before he is ready to write her book.

"I try to tell the story as she would tell it," he said. "If she hates men and is trying to get even with them in her book, that's the way I write it. If a woman wants to make her book sexy, and many of them do, I try to help, but I tone it down if they want to go too far.

"It's interesting when I work with them that many of these women look on me as a confessor and reveal their most intimate personal experiences. Sometimes when they're too intimate I suggest they write a novel rather than an autobiography. Most of the women I've written books for want to write about themselves in one way or another."

Mr. Michelson charges anywhere from $1,500 to $4,000 to ghost-write a book for a woman, depending on the length. He takes no responsibility for seeing that it is published, he said. His job ends when he delivers the manuscript to the client.

Usually the woman, if she's got the money, has her book published by what is known as a "vanity publisher"; that is to say, a publisher who will print the book, providing the author guarantees to buy 2,000 copies of it, which comes to about $1,500 or $2,000. Vanity publishing has become quite a big business. Many such publishers will not only arrange to have the book published, but will also set up the literary cocktail party to launch the work, and even see that the book is reviewed by a resident critic.

It is the cocktail party, the autograph signing, and the review that makes the time, effort, and expense of "writing" a book so worth while. In some cases a woman has been so happy with her first "book" that she's hired Mr. Michelson to write a second for her. This is especially true in cases where the neighbors have commented with envy that "she has only one good book in her."

Mr. Michelson says he rarely meets the husbands of the women he writes books for. Many of his clients come to his office, though he will go out of town to meet with the "author" if she pays his expenses.

He told me a lady from Dallas sneaks up to New York occasionally, ostensibly on a week's shopping trip. She really comes to write a book. Her husband has no idea what she's up to and she's constantly surprising him with a new "novel."

Mr. Michelson works on two or three books at the same time. He says there is a pattern to ghost-written books and that most women who have a story to tell want to put down on paper in one way or another that men are no damn good.

Raising Cultural Money

THERE HAS BEEN a lot of talk about building a National Cultural Center in Washington, D. C. The sum everyone is bandying about is thirty-two million dollars, and they're trying to raise the money around the country.

The first attempt at fund-raising was a closed-circuit television show and $100-a-plate dinner at the Washington Armory and other points throughout the country. It was very difficult for me to hear anything at the armory, except for some very uncultured remarks about the acoustics from the people who sat at the next table.

They put the arm on every businessman in Washington for the dinner and there was a certain amount of resentment about it. One man said, "They should have given us an option. If you wanted to give one hundred dollars to the Center, you had to come to dinner, but if you wanted to give two hundred, you should have been allowed to stay at home."

The trouble with building a cultural center in Washington is that most of the country feels Washington should build its own cultural center without help from the colonies. But there aren't that many people in Washington with thirty-two million dollars to spare, and since the people behind the National Cultural Center say it will be for all Americans, they feel everyone should help.

The real problem is both sides are right. Actually Congress should provide the money for a cultural center, but unfortunately they've just voted ten million dollars for an aquarium, so it's very difficult to get any more funds out of Congress for something as useless as a cultural center. Nobody really wanted an aquarium in Washington, D. C., except a very powerful congressman from Ohio named Michael Kirwan of the Appropriations Committee.

You see, ever since he was a little boy, Congressman Kirwan loved fish, and he was real upset because the kids in Washington had no aquarium to go to. Of course, the kids in Washington hardly have enough schools to go to, and there is a shortage of hospitals and police protection in the nation's capital, but Congressman Kirwan felt an aquarium came first. Since he had a lot to say about who would get appropriations for other projects in the country, Congress fell in line and gave him ten million dollars for the aquarium.

Actually, the House of Representatives voted twenty million dollars for the aquarium, but the penny-pinching Senate threw cold water on the bill and only gave him ten million dollars. The congressmen and Senators who voted for the bill could sleep at night because they justified it this way. They work very hard and there is nothing more peaceful than an aquarium to get away from it all. A cultural center is noisy, there is always someone playing some instrument or singing or making a racket of some kind. But fish don't make any noise and therefore an aquarium fits into Washington life better than a cultural center.

So that's why the American people are being asked to contribute to the National Cultural Center. There is just so much money Congress can give Washington, and this year it's all going to fish.

But there is one bright spot. As soon as the aquarium is built, it could be used occasionally as a cultural center for concerts and dramatic performances. I understand from a dolphin the acoustics at an aquarium are not bad at all.

Composer Can't Bank on Getting a Loan

EVERYONE TALKS about culture in America, but Irwin Bazelon, an American composer, is not sure anyone wants to do anything about it.

"A lot of money is being raised for buildings," Bazelon told me, "but very little money is being put aside for live American composers."

This irks the forty-year-old composer, who came to Washington to conduct a piece he wrote, "Testimonial to a Big City," with the National Symphony Orchestra.

Bazelon told me that when he really gets depressed, he amuses himself by trying to get a personal loan from a bank.

"What I do is I go into the bank and tell someone I want to get a loan. They're usually very nice to me—at first. I'm ushered to the assistant to the assistant vice-president's desk and the questioning begins.

" 'What do you do for a living?' the bank man asks.

" 'I'm a composer,' I reply.

" 'Oh, you write songs?' he says, still being very friendly.

" 'No,' I say, 'I write chamber music and symphonies.'

"Now he looks at me as if I'm a real nut. 'But how do you make a living?'

" 'Sometimes I write music for television, sometimes for documentaries, and occasionally I write for a producer.'

" 'Well, what have you done in the last two months?'

" 'I've been working on a symphony.'

" 'How much did you make writing it?'

" 'I didn't make anything. That's why I came here for a loan.'

" 'How much did you make last year?' he asks.

" 'I don't know. Maybe three thousand dollars.'

" 'And the year before?'

" 'Maybe two thousand.'

"By now the assistant is really confused, so he calls for the assistant vice-president, who also is very friendly at the beginning. He says to me, 'What do you want the loan for—a car or home improvement?'

"I say, 'I want the money to eat with, maybe pay my rent.'

"And he says, 'Well, we really can't lend you money for that.'

"Then he says, 'Do you have any collateral?'

"At this point I produce three of the symphonies I've written. 'Here, I'll put these up for collateral.'

" 'But,' he cries, 'we can't put any value on these.'

" 'Why not?' I cry. 'Are you trying to tell me a symphony isn't worth anything?'

"The assistant vice-president calls for the vice-president.

"The vice-president says, 'Look, if you get a commission to write some music for somebody, bring it in and we'll give you a loan against it.'

" 'But,' I say, 'if I had a commision to write something, I wouldn't need a loan. I want the money to tide me over between commissions.'

"Now I've got them all in a frenzy. A kid delivering coffee and sandwiches across the street can get a loan, a secretary can get a loan, a ditchdigger can get a loan. But they don't know what to do with an American composer.

"Everybody's upset. Then I say, 'I have an idea. Instead of a loan, why doesn't the bank commission me to write a piece of music? Everybody thinks banks are cold and don't have a heart. If you commission me to write a piece, I won't need the loan.'

"The vice-president starts shaking. 'We can't commission you to write a piece of music.'

" 'Why not? You have plenty of money. Don't you think you should use some of it to support the arts?'

"To get rid of me they usually say, 'We'll call you about it. Just leave your phone number.'

"I know they have no intention of calling me, but it doesn't matter. I have spent a pleasant afternoon and shaken up a bank with assets of over one hundred million dollars. American composers may be poor, but that doesn't mean they can't have a little fun."

The Piano

"WHAT'S HAPPENED TO US?" I asked my wife the other day when we were both lying in bed.

"What do you mean, 'What's happened to us?'"

"I mean here we are with a nice home, and three lovely children and we never do anything together."

"We eat together," she said.

"I don't mean that. I mean we never do things like sit around the piano in the evening and sing family songs."

"We don't have a piano," she said.

"Now you're being technical. We could buy a piano."

"Who would play it?" she wanted to know.

"They have them now with paper rollers. Electric ones. All you do is push a button and it plays 'Long Long Trail A-winding' all by itself."

"I'm not interested. I'd rather have a new rug for the living room."

"You're always thinking of material things. What about the spiritual side of our lives. Our children will grow up and have no memories of us at all. We're a family group and we should do things as a family."

"The children would rather watch television."

"Of course they would. That's just it. We've got to get them away from the TV set."

"With an electric piano?"

"Yes, if need be, with an electric piano."

"Why can't we all sing along with Mitch?"

"Very funny. But don't try to stop me. A family that sings together, swings together."

"I still would rather have a rug."

The next day I went down to the piano store, and for eleven hundred dollars—one hundred down and sixty-five a month—bought a beautiful electric piano with thirty rolls of songs. It was delivered three days later and you should have heard the shouts of excitement when it arrived. The children were thrilled and couldn't wait to push the electric buttons.

"You see, Mother," I said to my wife, "if you give children the choice of doing things together or watching television, they'll always choose the former."

That night the family gathered in the living room and as I sat at the pedals we all sang 'Long Long Trail A-winding,' 'The Old Oaken Bucket,' and 'Red River Valley.' Tears came to my eyes as I looked around me and saw my family singing to their hearts' content. We could have sung all night, but I didn't want to overdo it.

"Tomorrow night we'll do the same thing," I promised, as they went merrily off to bed.

The next evening after supper I said, "Now everybody into the living room."

"I've got to do my homework," Joel, my nine-year-old, said.

"You never wanted to do your homework before," I said angrily.

"Stop shouting," my wife said. "If he wants to do his homework, don't stop him."

"I don't feel well," Connie, my eight-year-old, said.

"You looked perfectly well eating that second helping of ice cream," I cried.

"I'm sleepy," said Jennifer, the seven-year-old.

"It's only seven o'clock," I protested.

"I get tired early," she replied.

"Well, Mother. Would you like to sing with me?"

"I've got to hem the girls' dresses."

"But I've just put eleven hundred dollars into a new piano."

"I told you I would rather have a new rug," my wife said.

I went into the living room by myself and turned on the piano. I tried to sing "Shenandoah" all by myself but it just wasn't the same thing.

Ever since then the piano has been sitting in the living room gathering dust. But I guess I shouldn't complain. Joel does his homework every night now, Connie gets sick right after dinner, Jennifer goes to bed an hour before her regular bedtime, and my wife has been sewing like mad.

What do I do with my evenings? Well usually I watch *Dobie Gillis* or *Perry Mason*—any TV show, as long as it doesn't have a piano in it.

Confessions of a Tea-Bag-Tag Collector

AMERICA IS PROBABLY the most hobby-conscious country in the world. Anyone who doesn't have an outside interest is looked on with suspicion and contempt. We are a nation of collectors, traders and buyers whether it be art, stamps, guns, or automobiles.

Unfortunately most hobbies can get expensive and so when a friend of mine, a struggling song writer named Avery Corman, was forced into starting a hobby, by all his hobby-oriented friends, he decided to collect something that would be within his economic bracket—he decided to collect tea-bag tags.

Now tea-bag-tag collecting is a very rare hobby in the United States mainly because so many people drink coffee, and as far as I know there are no tea-bag-tag catalogues, nor is there a big market for rare tea-bag tags. People like Mr. Corman collect tea-bag tags for the personal pleasure they get out of it, rather than for the glory and status that comes with so many other American hobbies.

When Mr. Corman first started his hobby, about a year

and a half ago, he had a great decision to make. Should he collect the bag as well as the tag? He decided to play it safe and just collect the tag, particularly since all tea bags, once they're used, look alike.

Mr. Corman set up several rules for his hobby. He only collects tea-bag tags from tea that he himself has drunk. He is not interested in friends giving him tea-bag tags, nor does he want to trade in tea-bag tags.

"To me," he explained, "drinking tea is a very personal thing, and the tags I collect have value because I found them myself. If I started accepting tea-bag tags from others, the next step would be to start trading in them or collecting them in quantity. But that isn't the reason I collect them. I collect them because later on when I look at them I know that with each tag came a cup of tea that I drank myself. It gives me a sense of accomplishment and nostalgia and personal involvement which I think is the requisite a person should have for any hobby. Each tag represents a record of my tea-drinking experience, and therefore what is the sense of collecting tea-bag tags of tea that was drunk by other people? If someone has more tags than I have, I can only hope he gets as much pleasure out of his as I get out of mine. And I also hope that for his own self-respect he doesn't cheat and take them from other people.

"I'll admit that I have been tempted at times to accept a rare tea-bag tag from someone who had been to Hong Kong or India, but at the last minute I decided if I accepted one, then I would open the door to tea-bag-tag cheating and I don't know where my hobby would have led me."

Mr. Corman is an avid tea drinker because he feels you have some control over tea, while you have none over coffee.

"When you're served a cup of coffee, you have nothing to do. It's *their* cup of coffee. But when you order tea, you're creating from nothing. You have a virgin cup of hot water with a tea bag on the side. It's up to you to take these raw elements and make something of them. Not only must you know how long to leave the tea bag in the hot water, but you must also have the digital dexterity to remove the bag at the right moment without slopping any of the water into the saucer or onto your clothes. I have become so skillful at it that I can remove the bag from the cup at the same moment I remove the tag from the string. The risks involved with teamaking are very exciting and there is peril in every cup.

"Coffee drinkers have only to decide whether they want sugar or cream. What kind of experience can you have in making a decision like that?"

Since Mr. Corman collects tags he doesn't care much for brewed tea. "When you're served brewed tea, you're in a class with the coffee drinker. There's nothing creative involved in drinking brewed tea, and I get little pleasure out of it."

He told me that coffee drinkers have nothing to show for it after they've drunk a cup of coffee together. "But I come away with a tea-bag tag, so I haven't wasted my time."

Mr. Corman, who is twenty-seven years old, is a bachelor, but he says he's never used tea-bag tags as a lure to get a girl up to his apartment. "This would be defaming my hobby, and using my collection for something other than it is intended to be. Many of my girl friends don't even know I collect tea-bag tags. Very few of them would understand if I told them."

But one time Mr. Corman had a date with a girl for dinner.

"At the end of the meal," he said, "she ordered tea instead of coffee, and suddenly I noticed she started to remove the tag from the tea bag. My heart skipped a beat. Could she also be a tea-bag-tag collector? Could it be that we had found some fantastic rapport, and this was the woman I wanted for my wife?

" 'Why did you remove that tag from the tea bag?' I asked her excitedly.

" 'I was just nervous,' she replied.

"I then realized we had nothing in common. It seems I made her nervous, and what I thought was the real thing turned out to be nothing at all."

On TV Ratings

THE RECENT HEARINGS over television ratings have left the country in another moral quandary. For years I believed everything Mr. Nielsen and Mr. Trendex and Mr. Arbitron told me about the popularity of various television programs. By simply keeping track of one family's watching habits and multiplying it by something like 254,350, we all knew what were the successful and unsuccessful shows in the nation.

In the case of Nielsen, 1,200 families were used to tell us what 180,000,000 people were or were not watching at any moment. If one of those families went to visit their relatives on a specific night, that meant 150,000 families went to visit their relatives on the same evening.

It's no wonder television producers, advertisers, and network executives have been thrown into a spin by the hearings. They're determined to give the people what they want, but now they're not sure what the people are really looking at.

Last Sunday I decided to help out the poor TV industry and I monitored what my family watched during the day and night. If the executives of our great networks will multiply my home by 4,333,000, they'll have a good idea of what was watched last Sunday in homes throughout the country.

We have two TV sets in the house, one in our bedroom and one in the children's playroom, so I think I can give the TV industry a fair sampling.

Nobody watched any television Sunday morning, for one simple reason. There was an Easter-egg hunt in and around the house. Two eggs were hidden behind the television set, but you couldn't honestly call that watching anything.

At noon my nine-year-old son turned on *Championship Bowling*. His seven-year-old sister immediately turned to a show called *Wonderama*. My son slugged his sister. She slugged him back. My wife rushed into the room and said, "All right, if you can't watch television without fighting, no one can look at it." And she turned the set off.

At three o'clock I decided to watch *Challenger Golf* with Arnold Palmer and Jack Nicklaus. But as soon as I turned on the set my son complained to his mother, "If we can't watch television, then why can Daddy?"

My wife asked me to turn off the set so I wouldn't upset the children.

Six-thirty rolled around and my wife's embargo on TV was lifted. I turned on *Meet the Press*, but my six-year-old daughter came into the room and switched on *Mister Ed*.

"Joel and Connie want to watch *McKeever and the Colonel*," she said. "And I want to watch *Mister Ed*."

So I didn't get to watch *Meet the Press*.

At seven we all had dinner and the sets were turned off. The children misbehaved at dinner so their mother said, "No television after dinner. You all go straight to bed."

"Does that include me?" I asked.

"You've got to fix the kitchen door or it will fall on someone. You've promised me you'd do it two Sundays in a row."

It took me two hours to fix the door. Then I looked up the television schedule and discovered Bob Hope was on. Just as I got Bob Hope tuned in, the telephone rang. It was my mother-in-law calling my wife to wish her a happy Easter.

"Would you turn the set off?" my wife asked. "I can't hear a word Mother is saying."

So I heard every word her mother said for an hour.

When my wife hung up, I turned on Dinah Shore—but not for long. My son walked in and complained the set was playing too loud and he couldn't go to sleep.

"Turn down the TV," my wife said.

"If I turn down the set I can't hear Dinah Shore sing," I protested.

"Well, he's got to get some sleep."

I turned the set off until eleven o'clock. Then I turned on Wallace Beery in an old movie, *This Man's Navy*, but just as the titles came on the screen I fell asleep. My wife told me the next morning she turned off the set five minutes later.

That is an accurate diary of one family's TV viewing habits. By multiplying all this data, the TV executives can start canceling their Sunday programs right now.

The Curse of the Zebu

WHEN PEOPLE ASK me if I miss French food in Washington, I have to admit I do, up to a point. But then there is always the National Zoological Restaurant in Washington, where an organization called the Anteaters' Association serves, at certain rare times of the year, such exotic dishes as roast hippopotamus, royal zebu, Canada honker, and fried aoudad, to name but a few. The Anteaters dine on zoological specialties from all over the world, and one year you can find yourself eating bear's paw, the next year whale blubber, the next wild buffalo rump or filet of iguana.

I went to the zoo restaurant last November as the guest of Gordon Leach, who started the Anteaters eighteen years ago and also runs the restaurant as a concession. The *plat du jour* was royal Indian zebu, cut from the hindquarters of the sacred Brahma cattle. Zebu is very delicious, and, for those who have never tried it, it tastes a little like hippopotamus. As a matter of fact, it is so tasty that it is forbidden to be eaten in certain parts of the world, and some say if you partake of zebu you run the risk of angering the gods, who could bring a curse down on you. I, of course, laughed at this because in the United States we're above such gastronomic threats.

Before the zebu I was treated to a piece of aoudad, the wild sheep that hides high in the mountains of Africa. Aoudad (pronounced, "Who is that?") is about the toughest kind of sheep you can eat, and just one tidbit is enough to make you cry for zebu.

I ate the zebu with relish, and washed it down with a strong red burgundy from the jungles of France. I topped off the lunch with custard and black African coffee.

I thanked Mr. Leach for everything but the aoudad, and asked him to call me a taxi. Then I went outside in the freezing cold to wait for the cab. Forty-five minutes later I was still waiting. I called the taxi company and complained of the wait to the dispatcher, who said angrily: "I only dispatch taxis. I can't help it if they don't show up." Could the curse of the zebu be upon me? No, it was ridiculous.

An hour later a taxi finally showed up and I rode to the office. But when I got there my secretary was gone. She came in at 3:30 complaining she had been held up by the hairdresser. At four I received a call from a woman who said I had not bought any hundred-dollar tickets for the National Culture Center dinner at the armory. Maybe there was something to the zebu curse after all.

I put it out of my mind until I tried to get a taxi to go home that night. It took me over an hour to find one. When I arrived home I found my wife in tears. It seems our new electric oven, which was supposed to roast the Thanksgiving turkey on the following morning, had broken down and no one would come and fix it.

I tried to cheer her up as best I could. I pointed out that the guarantee on the oven was up last week, and the company who installed the oven probably pushed a button in their main headquarters so it wouldn't work on Thanksgiving Day.

"I can't even fix you supper," she sobbed.

"That's all right," I said, "I'm not hungry anyway. I had royal zebu for lunch."

"You ate zebu for lunch," she cried in horror. "Just before Thanksgiving?"

"Sure. It was quite good too."

"But what about the curse?" she asked.

"Oh, that's ridiculous. It's an old wives' tale."

"Well, what about the oven?" she cried. "Is that an old

wives' tale? And with my mother coming for Thanksgiving tomorrow."

"Your mother is coming for Thanksgiving?" I shouted. Now I was sure of it. The curse of the zebu had caught up with me after all.

Breathe Deeply

THERE IS A COMPANY in New York called Kelly Girl Service, Inc., which supplies temporary white-collar female workers for any kind of job that's within the law. The other day the executives of Kelly Girls were asked to supply twenty-four girls for a nasal decongestion company, the catch being the girls had to have head colds. It seems the decongestion company was putting a new product on the market (a decongestant spray that would clear up a whole room) and wanted to say that nine out of ten people who were tested with the decongestant found relief. The trouble was the nasal decongestion company was having difficulty finding people with colds, and therefore turned over the job to Kelly Girl Service, Inc.

I went over to the office where girls were being interviewed for the work. A letter had gone out to all Kelly Girl workers urging them to respond if they had a cold or knew of someone who had one. The morning I arrived seven girls were waiting to be interviewed and the phones were ringing like mad.

In charge of the project was Miss Lila Howard, who, after she screened the candidates, sent them up to a laboratory on 135th Street, where the girls would be paid two dollars an hour while they sat in a room breathing in the decongestant.

When I walked into her office Miss Howard was on the phone. "All right," she was saying, "but are you really congested? . . . I don't care if you have a sore throat. I need head colds . . . Is it really stuffed up? Well, I tell you what you do. Close your mouth and breathe in. Did any air get up? . . . No? . . . All right, come in. You may be a prospect."

Miss Howard, a very attractive young lady, told me, "This is the toughest assignment we've ever had. The trouble is, if you've got a bad head cold, the kind that the decongestant company wants, you don't want to get out of bed. And if you feel well enough to go out on a job, usually you're not congested enough."

"How do they know if you are congested enough or not?" I asked her.

"They have a machine. It's kind of a nasal lie detector. It measures your congestion. I've sent thirteen girls to the lab and only three were chosen. That shows you how serious this business is."

The phone rang again. Miss Howard picked it up. "No dear, a chest cold won't do. Just take a couple of aspirins and stay in bed."

"Yesterday," she told me, "a girl called, but she had such a bad case of laryngitis we never did get her name. My ear is getting attuned to head colds. I can almost tell over the phone now if a girl has it in her or not."

She continued, "The main problem is the weather has been good, and not too many people have colds."

Just then a girl was ushered in to Miss Howard. She sounded pretty stopped up. "Miss Howard," she said, "you said you would take anyone with a cold, so I gave my boy friend a cold and we'd like to go up together."

Miss Howard was thrilled. "What a wonderful spirit! If all Kelly girls were only like you!" She wrote something on a slip of paper and handed it to the girl. "And remember, don't take any medication. We want your cold just as it is."

Another lady entered. "I couldn't find the laboratory," she complained.

"Did you get off at the right subway station?"

"I don't know, but it was raining, and I decided there was no sense walking in it if I had a cold."

"But it could have helped. You might have become more congested."

"Yeh, but what good will decongestants do if I got pneumonia?"

When she left, Miss Howard said, "You see the difference. One girl is loyal and even gives her cold to her boy friend— the next one is afraid of catching pneumonia. That's what I've been up against all week."

The phone rang. "Yes, we are looking for colds," Miss Howard said. "Chronic sinus? It's possible . . . Can you breathe with your mouth closed? . . . You can . . . Oh, that's too bad . . . Well, call me back if you can't breathe. Thanks for calling and I sincerely hope you feel much worse."

6.

COLD WARS,
HOT LINES

At the Press Club Bar

EVERY TIME there is a serious crisis and I think things have worked out okay, I bump into this fellow who upsets the apple cart. You've probably met him yourself. He found me in the bar of the National Press Club, where I was celebrating the free world's latest victory over the forces of godless tyranny.

"Well," he said, slapping me on the back. "It looks like the Russians have to move their missile sites out of Cuba."

"That's good," I said happily.

"No, that's bad. This has been an awful blow to the Russians and they're going to have to react somewhere else to save face."

"That's bad," I said nervously.

"No, that's good," he said. "The Russians never thought we would act so forcefully in Cuba. It came as a complete surprise to Khrushchev."

"That's good," I said, my spirits rising.

"No, that's bad. Khrushchev may be in a spot now in the Kremlin with the rest of his Presidium for this defeat, and may even be kicked out because of it. We could get someone much worse than Khrushchev if we're not careful."

"That would be bad," I agreed.

"It could be good," he said. "If they're fighting among themselves, they may not have time to make any new move against us."

"That's good," I said, almost ready to buy him a drink.

"No, that's bad, because we don't know the role the Red Army played in all this. This may be the time the military tries to take over."

"That's bad," I said, deciding not to buy him a drink.

"I'm not so sure," he said. "It's quite possible the military has been discredited in the Kremlin, and Khrushchev is riding higher than ever."

"Is that good or bad?" I asked, deciding to sit on the fence.

"It all depends on what China does. China may now decide to help Castro."

"Well, I know that's bad," I said with conviction.

"I wouldn't be too sure," he replied. "The sooner Khru-shchev and Communist China break completely, the better it will be for the West."

"I can see where that would be good."

"But it could be bad," he said. "If we have nuclear disarma-ment and then China gets its own atomic weapons, Russia as well as the United States would be in the soup."

"That's bad," I said, trying not to get too depressed.

"But we can't overlook the good side. If Russia decides that China is bad for them, she may be forced into getting along with us."

"That's good," I said.

"It would be if someone knew what to do about Castro."

"He's bad," I said.

"And yet he's been good for us," the man said. "We wouldn't have thought of helping the South American countries if it hadn't been for Castro."

"Good for Castro," I heard myself saying.

"But we're dealing with a nut in Cuba, and that's always bad."

"I can see where that's no good," I said. "What do you suggest?"

"Well, there's always the Monroe Doctrine."

"That's good," I said.

"That's bad, because we're the only ones who think the Monroe Doctrine has any validity."

"Then why did you bring it up?" I said bitterly.

"Because we've decided to act unilaterally if our interests are endangered in this hemisphere."

"That's good," I said.

"Ah, yes, but this might open up a new can of beans, and the Russians might decide to act unilaterally somewhere else."

I started to cry.

"Now don't take it so hard," he said. "Don't forget in times like these, war is unthinkable."

"That's good," I said, taking out my handkerchief.

"At least it was until last week."

And that's when I hit him. It was a unilateral act, but I had the support of everybody at the bar.

A New Bulgarian Cigarette

I READ THE OTHER DAY where the Bulgarians, of all people, have developed a new cigarette called "Atrotabak." The cigarettes are said to contain no nicotine, but have other active ingredients which help in the curing of bronchial asthma, duodenal ulcers, and high blood pressure.

One of the ingredients in the new cigarette is scopolamine, otherwise known as the truth drug, which it is said makes one tell all. Needless to add, the introduction of scopolamine in cigarettes could cause many complications.

Just think of what is happening in Bulgaria right at this moment. Ivan Donovich, suffering from an ulcer, goes to his doctor.

"Apparently, Ivan," the doctor says, "you've been smoking more but enjoying it less. I'm going to recommend a new cigarette for you. Take one before meals and one after meals, and double the dose on Sundays. I don't like the look of that ulcer."

Ivan goes out and buys several packs of Atrotabaks and follows the doctor's instructions. In a month he is a new man. His ulcer is gone, his blood pressure is down, and he has no bronchial asthma. He returns to the doctor in high spirits.

"Just as I thought," the doctor says, "Atrotabaks did the trick. Any side effects?"

"None at all," says Ivan, "except I had to wait two hours in front of that lousy state-owned tobacco shop to buy one stinking pack of cigarettes."

"Ah," says the doctor, "you don't like the Communist form of distribution of goods."

"You can say that again, Doc. The system stinks. And if you want to know the truth, so do the Communists. I liked it much better in this country before the lousy Reds took over."

The doctor holds out a pack of cigarettes and says to Ivan, "Cigarette, Ivan?"

"Don't mind if I do." Ivan takes one. "And let me tell you something else, Doc. Don't think the people are going to stand for it much longer. One of these days we're all going to say the heck with it and—bam!"

"You're getting ashes on the floor, Ivan. How do you propose to go 'bam'?"

"Counterrevolution. Mmmmmnn, these Atrotabaks taste good like a cigarette should. And they're so mild."

"But even with the mildness they still have cigarette flavor," the doctor says. "Do you have any friends who think the way you do?"

"Sure I do. All of us down at the steel mill are ready to throw over the regime. We just need a few guns and tanks and we move."

"Very interesting, Ivan. Do you have the names of your other conspirators?"

"Sure, Doc. I'd be happy to give them to you."

Ivan names all his friends.

The doctor writes out another prescription and hands it to Ivan.

"What's this for?"

"The secret police, Ivan. You're under arrest as an enemy of the state."

Two burly plain-clothes policemen come in and drag Ivan

away. His trial is swift and he is sentenced to be shot before a firing squad. Just before he is blindfolded, the captain comes up to him.

"You can have a last cigarette. Would you care for an Atrotabak?"

"No, sir. I'm changing brands. I'll take a Dudnidnok. At least the only thing they give you is cancer."

So Let's Snub Them

WHEN UNDERSECRETARY of state for Political Affairs Averell Harriman went to Moscow recently to discuss the Laos problem with the Russians, it was reported that he received a cool reception from Soviet officials. A very minor deputy from the Protocol Office met Mr. Harriman when he got off the plane in Moscow, and everyone feels that because of the Undersecretary's rank, and the fact he was bringing a message from President Kennedy, he should have been greeted by at least the Deputy Foreign Minister or by Khrushchev's son-in-law.

Well, if the Russians want to play dirty pool when it comes to protocol, I think the United States should reciprocate. I strongly urge our State Department to appoint an Assistant Secretary for Snubbing Foreign Diplomats. His function would be to treat diplomats of countries who have snubbed our diplomats with contempt and coolness.

If, for example, a high Russian official comes to Washington, D. C., in the near future, the Assistant Secretary would see to it that a dirty red carpet was rolled out to his plane. To show we really meant business, the official would be greeted by only one person—the boy who parks the cars at the Howard Johnson motel. Speeches would be held to a minimum. The official would be taken into town from the airport in a regular air-line bus and deposited at the air-line terminal, where he could make his own way to Blair House.

Since Mr. Harriman was ignored by the Soviet press and radio, the American press would be urged not to say anything about the Russian official's arrival. Editors would be urged as a matter of national urgency to refrain from printing his photograph, and David Susskind would be asked—as a patriotic gesture—not to interview him on television.

Other steps to ignore the Russian official could be taken. If for any reason he had to go to the White House, he would not be allowed to shake hands with Caroline or John Kennedy, Jr. All state functions would be held to a minimum. If the State Department felt it had to give him a luncheon, it would be held in the State Department cafeteria with a few minor typists and mimeograph operators in attendance.

The Assistant Secretary in Charge of Snubbing Foreign Diplomats would see to it that the Russian official was kept waiting for all appointments, and when he requested to see an American official, that official would always be out to lunch. If the Russian diplomat called anyone, he would be told the person would call him back, which of course would not be the case.

It's possible the Russian might bring his wife with him. If so, she would not be allowed to visit any children's hospitals, have tea with Mrs. Lyndon Johnson, or go shopping at Garfinckel's for her grandchildren.

Everyone would behave correctly but coolly.

This is just a rough plan. A lot of refinements for snubbing foreign officials could be worked out by the Assistant Secretary and his staff. But I do believe that after a couple of visits the Soviets would think twice about snubbing an American Undersecretary of State.

We may stand for Russian troops in Cuba, but the American people are not going to tolerate the Soviets turning their backs on Averell Harriman.

They Need Each Other

EVERY TIME things get quiet, or comparatively quiet, between East and West, the rumors start flying that Khrushchev is on his way out and that there is a new struggle in the Kremlin for power. In our own country when things quiet down, the rumors have it that President Kennedy will have no chance of getting his program through, and he is certain of being cut down on all his requests.

The sad fact, whether they like it or not, is that Khrushchev needs Kennedy and Kennedy needs Khrushchev, and I wouldn't be surprised if the "hot line" between Moscow and Washington serves a purpose other than to prevent accidental war.

I can imagine a conversation taking place between the two heads of state that might go something like this.

"Mr. Khrushchev, I'm sorry to bother you, but I was wondering when you were planning to send another man in orbit. I'm having a helluva time getting space funds. Is there any chance of getting a Russian up in space in the next two months?"

"We've been trying, but we've had some setbacks. You haven't been helping me much, you know, by postponing Cooper's flight. I'm having difficulty on funds also."

"I'm sorry about Cooper, Mr. Khrushchev, but we've had trouble with our booster. If you could send two or three men up right now, I'll do something spectacular for you when your next budget comes up."

"I'll see what I can do, Mr. Kennedy. By the way, you would be helping me quite a bit if you announced you were going to ring the Soviet Union with Polaris submarines."

"How's that?"

"The Soviet Navy is having a fight for appropriations with the Soviet Army and Air Force, and a threat from you might help Soviet naval morale quite a bit."

"But, Mr. Khrushchev, I just announced we were giving Polaris missiles to our NATO forces. Isn't that enough?"

"Make it a little stronger."

"I don't want to go overboard."

"May I remind you, Mr. Kennedy, that if it weren't for Soviet troops in Cuba you would be having a great deal of trouble with your military appropriations. If you're not willing to help me out on the submarines, I might be forced to withdraw all my troops from Cuba."

"No, don't do that, Mr. Khrushchev. But as long as we're asking favors, I'd like to point out to you that because of the Communist failure to subvert many neutral countries I doubt if I'll get my foreign-aid bill through this year."

"We're doing the best we can for you in Viet-Nam, Mr. Kennedy."

"That's military. What happened to you in Italy and France and the Congo?

"I'll admit we haven't been doing so well there, but you haven't helped me much by continuing the disarmament talks. They cut my atomic-energy program by ten billion rubles because of your compromise on onsite inspections."

"I'm sorry about that, Mr. Khrushchev. But I was sure you wouldn't agree to them, anyway, so I went ahead with the proposal."

"Well, I wish you'd check with me first, Mr. Kennedy. Oh, by the way, we're announcing a new antimissile missile which will go into production in the fall."

"I'm happy to hear it. Our antimissile missile program has been lagging and this will certainly give it a good jab in the arm. Thanks a lot."

"Don't mention it. I'm having trouble, though, getting authorization for some more ground divisions. Could you possibly have your General Taylor make a speech about brush-fire wars again?"

"Will do. It's been nice talking to you."

"Same here. My best to Mrs. Kennedy."

Protect Us from Our Friends

"THAT BLANKETY-BLANK," said my friend from the New Frontier, "he's not going to get away with it. You can push us so far, and then we're going to start doing some pushing on our own."

"Who are you talking about? Castro?" I asked him.

"No, of course not. I'm talking about de Gaulle," he replied.

"Oh."

"And don't think we're going to take it lying down. They depend on us as much as we depend on them, and we have to stick together whether we like it or not."

"Are you talking about the French?"

"No, stupid, I'm talking about the Canadians. You would think they would see the importance of nuclear weapons in our defense setup."

"You might think they would learn from experience," I said, since it sounded like the right thing to say.

"I don't care about the larger powers. They can fend for themselves. It's the little countries I'm worried about. They're the ones we've committed our support to."

"You mean countries like Denmark?" I asked.

"No, I mean countries like Great Britain. They look up to us and we can't let them down."

"I never thought of it that way, but you're right," I said.

"When I think of all the time and effort we put into our Polaris submarines and now no one wants them, it makes my blood boil."

"Israel wants them," I said.

"Israel isn't being threatened by communism—just Arabs," he replied. "We've got to put the stuff where it will do us some good. Well, at least there is one country that appreciates what we're doing."

"West Germany?"

"Of course not. India. Now there is a friend. They're willing to let us defend them. They'll even take American troops if we send them. None of this hemming and hawing about what weapons they will or will not accept. If only the French were as easy to get along with as the Indians."

"Indians are fine people," I said.

"It's the Chinese we have to be worried about," he told me. "Mark my words, they're going to cause trouble for us."

"The Communist Chinese are very dangerous."

"Who's talking about the Communist Chinese. I'm talking about the Taiwan Chinese. If we don't watch them, they'll launch an attack on the mainland, and then what the devil do we do?"

I agreed. "It sure is a tricky thing."

"And don't think there still isn't going to be trouble in Africa. We've got to watch them every minute or we'll really be in the soup."

"Who, the Katangans?"

"Hell, no, the Portuguese. Don't think the problems of Angola and Mozambique have been solved by a long shot."

"You always have to look over your shoulder," I said.

"They think they can stop us from doing what we started out to do, but they're wrong. If they don't accept our policy, we'll shove it down their throats."

"Are you talking about the Russians?"

"No, I mean the Eighty-eighth Congress, you idiot."

"I'm sorry, I forgot to buy a scorecard," I said.

"Well, at least we've learned something from all this."

"What's that?"

"If you have an ally for an ally, you don't need an enemy."

Why We Remained Calm

A LOT OF PEOPLE have been amazed at how calmly the American people took the Cuban crisis. There was little panic in spite of the fact that we were on the verge of nuclear war, and people, at least in Washington, kept their *sang-froid* to the bitter end.

I have a theory as to why no one went off the deep end or headed for the hills. We owe it all to the television commercials interspersed in the news programs and bulletins, which made us realize that no matter how near we came to obliteration, the real menace to Americans was not Soviet supply ships or Cuban missile bases, but acid indigestion, halitosis, headaches, and underarm perspiration.

This is how it went as we all sat glued to our television sets, hanging onto every word from our nation's army of commentators.

"Good evening, ladies and gentlemen. President Kennedy has just announced that the United States will set up a quarantine around the island of Cuba and will fire on any ship, Russian or otherwise, which tries to break through. But before that story, here is some good news for sufferers from sinus headaches."

A turning of the dial found us face to face with a grim-faced Pentagon reporter who said, "War or peace. That was the big question in the Pentagon tonight. The armed services are ready for all-out nuclear attacks, and we'll tell you more about it as soon as we bring you a message from someone who knows something about athlete's foot."

Since I didn't have athlete's foot, I turned the dial again and saw a man standing by a map ringed with battleships.

"This was the situation tonight," he said, pointing to Cuba. "Missile bases with offensive weapons are being built. We'll tell you where in just a moment, after an important announcement from the Glug Drug Company."

A woman came on the screen screaming at her child. "Why are you so nervous?" her friendly friend asked her.

"It's my head," the screaming mother said, holding it in both hands.

"I have just the thing for it," the friend said. "Six-way relief with twelve active ingredients."

I quickly switched to a fourth channel and heard the announcer say, "And from Moscow we have just received Premier Khrushchev's reaction to President Kennedy's quarantine order. We'll tell you about it in a minute, after this warning for motorists who can't believe that cold weather has arrived."

You can imagine my dilemma. Washington has only four channels, and I still couldn't find out what was going on, so I turned to the first channel again, only I was too late. The commentator said, "And that's all civil-defense experts would say about the shelters. Now, let's talk about overeating and what you're doing about it."

Furiously I switched again only to hear, ". . . Marines to Florida where an invasion was impending. Are you smoking more but enjoying it less? Maybe it's time you changed."

I started holding my head in my hands just like the woman in the commercial did. My wife walked in and said, "What's the latest?"

"Give me a cigarette," I screamed. "I've got a headache and I have to change my oil before there's a summit meeting and we're all blown up."

"You shouldn't watch the news if it gets you so nervous," she said.

"Who's nervous? Just because I perspire and I use greasy kid stuff on my hair and I suffer from acid indigestion, is that any reason they won't tell me what's going on?"

"You're exaggerating," she said, flipping the dial.

A face came on the screen and a man was saying, ". . . a thermonuclear war so devastating that President Kennedy said victory would be ashes in our mouths. And now let's hear a friendly message about loose dental plates."

The Hot Line

WHEN THE SOVIET UNION announced it was willing to accept a direct "hot-line" telecommunications link between the Kremlin and the White House to prevent an accidental outbreak of a world war, it opened a whole new era in diplomacy. Unfortunately, the way things are going in the world, you need more than one telephone to prevent accidental war.

If we're going to set up a hot line to the Kremlin, we also had better set up one with General de Gaulle. Not that General de Gaulle would answer the phone even if it did ring, but at least he couldn't say we didn't try to call him.

But let us suppose that there was a hot line to General de Gaulle from the White House, and let us suppose President Kennedy had to use it, and let us suppose General de Gaulle answered the phone.

"General de Gaulle, this is President Kennedy."

"Ah, Monsieur le Président, you have called to ask me once again to let the English join the Common Market. My answer is no."

"No, General, that is not why I called. It is something much more serious."

"You want us to take back Canada. The answer is no."

"General, it's more serious than that."

"You are making your brother Bobby Ambassador to France?"

"No, no, no. General, an atomic missile is heading your way!"

"It's about time."

"You don't understand, General. It was fired accidentally. We're not giving it to you; we're shooting it at you."

"Ah, *zut*. I knew I should have never answered the phone. Well, there is only one thing to do."

"What's that, General?"

"We must accidentally fire one at you."

"I was going to suggest that. You must have read *Fail-Safe*."

"It kept me awake all night."

"But, General, you don't have a missile that can reach the United States."

"That is a problem. Could we send it by bomber?"

"That would be much too slow. Our missile should reach you in about fifteen minutes."

"Ah, you Americans. All you can ever think of is speed. Why don't you take it easier and enjoy life?"

"General, you're not taking this seriously enough."

"Well, what do you suggest—a summit conference?"

"I just wanted to explain to you it was an accident. No matter what our differences in the past, we had no intention of shooting a missile at you."

"I am most grateful, Monsieur le Président. I would hate to think our attitude toward the Atlantic Alliance would have caused you to take such unilateral action."

"There is one slight chance, General. We're trying to reach the missile by radio. If we do we can blow it up over the Atlantic Ocean."

"That would be nice, too."

"Wait a minute, General. I think—yes, I think—they've done it! They blew it up in the air."

"*Voilà*, Monsieur le Président. America has saved France again. That's the part I can't stand. Every time we stop being eternally grateful to the United States, we have to start all over again."

A Variety of Birds for Castro's Beard

THERE HAS BEEN a lot of talk in Washington about who was a Dove and who was a Hawk during the Cuban crisis. A Dove, according to the *Saturday Evening Post,* was someone who was for a blockade of Cuba. A Hawk was someone who favored bombing the Russian missile bases.

It will come out sooner or later in some magazine piece, so I might as well confess right now, I wasn't a Dove or a Hawk —I was Chicken. It had nothing to do with the issues. I just didn't want to die.

When you look at it in retrospect, it was a very selfish attitude on my part, and as things turned out the Doves won. But that's because no one asked the Chickens what we would do.

As I saw it at the time, the thing to do in order to placate Khrushchev and make him get his missiles and planes out of Cuba was to make a trade with him. The Chickens were perfectly willing to give the Russians South Africa and Senator Ellender if they would just leave us alone in the Caribbean. If this wasn't enough, we were willing to throw in Nazi leader George Rockwell, at least a thousand members of the John Birch Society, and parts of Albania.

I'm sure Khrushchev would have gone for the deal, because as it turned out he didn't get anything at all and it cost him a lot of money to ship all that stuff there and home again.

Of course, in Washington everyone assumes that you were either a Dove or a Hawk, and the tougher the stand you took, the higher your prestige in the community. People who were Chickens now maintain they were Doves. Doves claim they were Hawks, and Hawks profess they were Eagles. To admit you were frightened during those tense hours is for the birds, and the only reason I'm doing it is I'm afraid someone high in the Administration is going to blow the whistle on me.

It may have been a mistake on my part, but during the height of the crisis, as the twenty-four Russian ships were approaching Cuba, I called up Pierre Salinger and said, "Pierre, I'm scared."

"Is that all you called me for?" he said.

"No, of course not," I said. "The reason I called is my wife's scared, too."

"And?"

"And the kids are scared."

"So?"

"I just thought the President would like to know where we stand."

All the Doves and Hawks have been ridiculing me, but I believe there were a lot more Chickens in the country than will stand up and be counted.

I don't mind being a Chicken, except it's kind of lonely. If you're a Dove or a Hawk and everything works out, you can take bows and tell everyone how right you were. But if you're a Chicken and things don't work out right, there won't be anybody left in Washington to talk to.

The Peril of Informing

ACCORDING TO A STORY in *The Nation,* an ex-FBI agent named Jack Levine let some top secrets out of the bag. Mr. Levine said that one fifth or 1,700 of the 8,500 members of the registered Communists in the United States were FBI informers. Mr. Levine said these 1,700 were dues-paying members, who gave the party its financial support. He also predicted that as Communist membership continues to decline and the percentage of informants increases, the day will soon come when FBI informants, who are rising rapidly to the top, will capture complete control of the party.

This is something that I'm sure Mr. J. Edgar Hoover never planned on, and if what Mr. Levine says is true, he will have to revise his whole book on Communist infiltration in the United States.

It isn't too farfetched to assume that in a couple of years the entire Communist Party will be made up of FBI inform- ants. The reason for this is that the Communists are very bad about paying their dues and the FBI informants are the only ones who have the money (provided, of course, by the FBI) to keep up their memberships.

Because they haven't paid their dues, the real Communists will be forced to leave the party, and the only ones left will be the FBI informants. Now one informant doesn't know who another informant is, so all the informants will assume the other informants are Communists. Yet in order to make his job pay off, the informant will have to justify his job and will, therefore, have to invent things to warrant his staying on the

FBI payroll. The informants will be in severe competition with each other and, as time goes on, their reports will become more dramatic as each one has to outdo the other.

As these reports pour into the FBI, each one more harrowing than the last, the Justice Department will have to take some action. What they'll probably do is hire more informants to keep tabs on the party.

The new informants will increase the Communist Party membership by 10,000, then 20,000, then 30,000 members, and pretty soon the party, which had been dying out, will get a new lease on life.

The trouble is that as the membership increases, the FBI will have to increase its vigilance and hire new informants to infiltrate the party. These new members, all dues-paying members, will, in order to keep it a secret that they are informants, have to prove they are Communists, and will have to get involved in subversive activities so they won't arouse suspicion.

Once these subversive activities are exposed, there will be a public outcry, and the FBI will have to send in more informants to show it is in control of the situation. Requests will be made for more funds from Congress and hearings will be held, at which time several of the informants, with paper bags over their faces, will testify to the danger of the increasing membership of the Communist Party.

Congress will authorize the money, urging the FBI to keep them informed of the dangers involved. In order to keep them informed, new informants will have to be recruited. In no time at all a million registered party members will be on the rolls, all paid for by the Department of Justice.

With so many informants the competition among them will get fierce. Informants will be forced to hand in longer and more complete reports. Evaluation teams will have to be set up all over the country. Each report will require new informants to check out the facts. In no time at all the Communists could become the leading political party in the country, and to show their strength would have to put up a candidate for the Presidency of the United States. And the name of the candidate? J. Edgar Hoover, of course. Who else?

Dream Interview with Richard Nixon

EVERY ONCE IN A WHILE, late at night when I'm tucked in bed, I shut my eyes and have a dream interview with some leading statesman or world figure who would not be available to me otherwise. One night I dreamed I interviewed former Vice-President Richard M. Nixon, who had just lost out in the gubernatorial race in California.

Mr. Nixon never looked better, and he was in wonderful spirits. He said, "I'm delighted to be able to talk to you, as I have the highest admiration for people in your profession."

"Then you're not upset about losing the election?"

"Heavens, no! In American politics it isn't who wins or loses but how we play the game that counts. I admire the way Governor Brown ran his campaign and I think he deserved to win."

"But don't you think he made some vicious charges against you and your family?"

"That's just politics. I never took the charges seriously. In this business you've got to have a sense of humor. I'm proud to say I never lost my temper once during the campaign and even in defeat I've been the first one to laugh."

"Sir, there have been rumors that you felt the press was unfair to you during the campaign and that they didn't report what you said accurately."

"Now where would a rumor like that ever start? Some of my best friends are newspapermen, and I think everyone leaned over backward to report my campaign without fear or prejudice. Without exception I have admired everything they have written about me, and I think my campaign was made so much more pleasant by having them with me during these difficult months."

"Do you feel that Governor Brown accused you of lack of patriotism or lack of heart during the contest?"

"What a ridiculous question! The one thing I admired about Governor Brown was that he never made any personal attacks on me, and I in turn never made any on him. The issues were quite clear from the start and they boiled down to one thing. 'Who was the best man for the job?' The people of California thought he was, and I would be a sore loser if I said that he questioned my patriotism during the campaign. Do you think I'm a sore loser?"

"Heck, no. Not in this dream anyway," I replied.

"Well, that's the kind of guy I am. I wouldn't want people to think otherwise."

"Do you think Governor Brown spent more money on his campaign than you did?"

"Maybe, but what difference does that make? I don't think money played an important part in this campaign. It was Cuba that probably caused all the difficulty. I was for the President's taking a strong stand in Cuba, but I didn't think he'd take it while I was running for office. The Communist threat was in California, not in Cuba, but people forgot about it out here. If the Russians had set up their missiles in Los Angeles, I think I would have won."

"Back to the press, sir. Someone quoted you as saying after you lost that the press wouldn't have Nixon to kick around any more. Would you like to elaborate on that?"

"I was misquoted," he replied. "I said 'stick around.' I was sorry the press wouldn't have Nixon to stick around any more."

"What are your plans now?" I asked him.

"Well, I might run for congressman, and if I lose, I might then run for State assemblyman, and if I lose that, I think I would make a good city councilor. I enjoy the give and take of politics, and besides it's the best way I can keep in touch with all my friends of the fourth estate."

Times Square Poll

I WAS STANDING in Times Square one day during the 1962 election campaign, held up by the police, because President Kennedy and Robert Morgenthau, the Democratic candidate for Governor of New York, were going to pass by. President Kennedy had flown all the way up to New York to give Mr. Morgenthau a helping hand in his campaign to defeat Governor Rockefeller. As I stood there I wondered if anyone changed his vote when he saw the President of the United States drive by in a convertible with a candidate sitting next to him.

Then, as luck would have it, I started talking to the man next to me, and I asked him whom he was planning to vote for.

"It all depends what happens in the next fifteen minutes," he said.

"How's that?" I asked him.

"I want to see what Morgenthau looks like. I never like to vote for a man I haven't seen."

"Then you are impressed by something like this?"

"Sure I am. What else is there to decide on?"

"Will the fact that the President is sitting in the car next to Mr. Morgenthau influence your thinking?"

"I haven't seen the President since 1960 and I want to get a look at him again."

"Did you come out especially to see the candidate today?"

"That's right. I saw Rockefeller at Coney Island some time ago. But I wanted to be fair to Morgenthau, so I came up here today. Frankly, I'd prefer a bigger parade. I'm just nuts about bands. Anybody who rides behind a good band can have my vote. Also ticker tape. I'm very interested in ticker tape. I believe the more ticker tape the candidate receives the better Governor he's going to be."

"That certainly is unusual," I had to admit. "Most people don't go into the issues as deeply as you have."

"If you're going to vote," he said, "you've got to have a certain responsibility. You don't just go to the booth and pull the lever. My wife is the same way. She wants to know what a candidate's wife looks like before she votes for him."

"Why isn't she here with you today?"

"Well, since Rockefeller doesn't have a wife this year, she's decided not to vote at all. Rockefeller's divorce kinda took the fun out of the campaign, as far as she was concerned."

Just then the crowd started to cheer and the President and Mr. Morgenthau rode slowly by, waving. The President waved to us, but Mr. Morgenthau was waving to the crowd on the other side of Forty-second Street.

"Well," I said to my friend as they disappeared, "what do you think?"

"Morgenthau made a mistake waving to those people on the other side. I didn't get a good look at his face."

"But the President waved at you," I said.

"Okay, so I'll vote for him in 1964. But I'm not sure about Morgenthau. I never trust a man who refuses to look me straight in the eye."

It's All in the Name

IT IS HARD AT THIS STAGE for us pundits to gauge the effect of Governor Rockefeller's voting strength after his divorce and new marriage to the former Mrs. Murphy.

I tried to get some idea of how the man in the street felt by calling my father, who represents a great cross section of the American public.

"Pop, do you think Rocky's chances have been hurt by his recent divorce and marriage?"

"Who? Rocky Marciano?"

"No, Rocky Rockefeller, the Governor of New York."

"You know him so well you can call him Rocky?" he wanted to know.

"I don't know him at all. Everyone calls him Rocky. It's like calling the President Jack."

"You call the President Jack?"

"No, at least not to his face. But when I'm out with a group of people I'll say, 'Did you hear what Jack said at his press conference?' Everyone in Washington does it."

"I don't think that's very polite. What do you call Mrs. Kennedy?"

"Jackie."

"Not even Jacqueline? You should be ashamed of yourself."

"Pop, Jackie is a term of endearment. If people call her Mrs. Kennedy that would mean they don't like her. Even Bobby is aware of that."

"Bobby who?"

I was becoming exasperated. "Bobby Kennedy. What's the matter with you, Pop? Are there any other Bobbies in the Government?"

"Mr. McNamara is not a Bobby?"

"He's a Bob, not a Bobby. There's a big difference. It's amazing how little the average layman understands about the inner workings of government."

"So what was your original question?" my father demanded.

"How do you feel about Rocky?"

"As opposed to whom?"

"To Barry or George. Do you think his marrying Happy will have any effect on his presidential aspirations?"

"Who's Happy?"

"That's Rocky's new wife."

"Her name's Happy?"

"It's a nickname, Pop. Her real name is Margaretta."

"So why don't you call her Margie?" he wanted to know.

"Because she prefers to be called Happy."

"She told you this?"

"No, I don't even know her. I never met her."

"You never met her and you're already calling her by her nickname?"

"Pop, you're being old-fashioned. In politics everyone is known by his first name. And their wives are known by their first names. Don't you remember Ike and Mamie, and Dick and Pat, and Harry and Bess, and Franklin and Eleanor?"

"Faces I remember. Names I have difficulty with."

"All right, then, what do you think of Governor Rockefeller's chances now that he's married to Mrs. Murphy?"

"That's better. I want you to have a little respect."

"But what about his chances?"

"All I can tell you is that I wasn't going to vote for him when he was married to the first Mrs. Rockefeller, I wasn't going to vote for him when he got divorced, and I don't plan on voting for him now."

"Why not?"

"I'm a Democrat, and I like the other fellow—what's-his-name?"

7.

UNMITIGATED
GAULLE

Love in Paris and Red Tape Too

OF ALL THE MEN I worked with on the Paris *Herald,* the one I admired the most was Milliken. Let me say right now that Milliken was not his real name, and I am using a false one only to protect the guilty, which Milliken certainly was.

Milliken was an American in his late twenties. He had a beard; he usually wore blue jeans and a torn sweater; he lived in a cold-water flat on the Left Bank; he was usually broke. And yet Milliken was always in the company of the most beautiful girls in Paris. They used to call him every day on my phone; they waited for him in front of the Paris *Herald* until midnight; they cooked breakfast for him; they let him use their bathtubs, and they lent him money until pay day. Milliken's cup was constantly running over.

I couldn't understand it and it drove me crazy. There had to be an answer somewhere. Finally after six months of taking his messages and watching him in operation, I could stand it no longer.

So one afternoon while we were having a drink at Fouquet's, on the Champs Elysées, I said, "Damn it all, Milliken, what's your secret? How do you get away with it?"

"Get away with what?" he said innocently.

"Get away with all these girls. You're not handsome, you're not rich, you don't even own a car. What right do you have to attract all these American women? What do they see in you?"

"It's quite simple," he said calmly. "No mystery about it at all. I promise to marry them."

"You what?"

"I promise to marry them. Once I promise to marry them, everything else comes easily."

"I don't get it," I said.

"All right, I'll explain it to you. Where did you get married?"

"In London."

"Why?" he asked.

"Because there is too much red tape for a foreigner who wants to get married in France. I waited four months and finally gave up."

"Exactly," said Milliken. "It's almost impossible for a foreigner to get married in France, so when I propose to a girl and we go down to the Prefect of Police to make an application for a marriage license, I know we'll never get it. But the girl doesn't know that, and while we're waiting for our papers to be processed, which they never will be, we're officially 'engaged.' And since I have proved I intend to marry the girl, she has no choice but to treat me as she would her future husband."

"Milliken, you're a rat," I said, trying to hide the awe in my voice.

"I am not a rat. The French bureaucrats are the rats. I am only taking advantage of an impossible governmental situation. I didn't make the loophole, but as with taxes, I have every right to make the most of it."

"But when does the girl wise up that you aren't going to marry her?"

"One month, maybe two months, maybe three, depending on how many times we visit the Prefect of Police. The more times we go down, the more discouraged she gets. But I must say I've never been blamed by any of them. They know I have no control over the French attitude toward foreigners getting married in France."

"It's an unbeatable system." I whistled.

"Too bad you went to London" was all he said to me.

During the next six months Milliken proposed to at least five girls that I knew of, and I watched him with the envy of a man who sees someone rolling nothing but sevens at a crap table.

But then one day Milliken came rushing into the office, his

face white, his hands shaking, stark fear in his eyes. "You've got to help me," he cried.

"What happened?"

"I proposed to this girl, a mousy one at that, last night, and this morning we went down to the Prefect of Police to apply for permission to get married and they're going to give it to us."

"It's impossible," I said.

"No, it isn't. The lady behind the counter said she didn't believe in red tape and if two people wanted to get married it was all she cared about. She's a crazy romantic."

"What can I do to help you?"

"Don't you know someone at the Prefect of Police who can stop it?"

"No, I don't."

"Well, come down with me this afternoon and tell them I'm married already, or I'm a deserter from the Army, or anything. You've got to save me."

I felt so sorry for Milliken I went down with him and his mousy fiancée to the Prefect.

"Voilà, Monsieur," the lady said. "I have all your papers."

The mouse screeched with joy.

"But I don't have my birth certificate," Milliken protested.

"Your passport will do."

"I better take a health examination."

"You look very healthy to me," the lady said.

"I'm married already," Milliken cried.

"Will you swear to that under oath?"

"No," said Milliken, "but he will." He pointed to me.

"The devil I will," I said.

"Then let's have no more nonsense, Monsieur," said the lady. "Marriage is a serious business and I have risked my job to see your papers were approved. Usually it would take months to get the permissions, but because you are both young and Americans, I have made an exception. Perhaps when they find out what I have done they will transfer me. But love is more important than the government."

Milliken was in a state of shock during the following week so I made all the arrangements at the local city hall for the wedding. I was Milliken's best man, my wife stood witness for the mouse. The mayor of the *arrondissement* made a beautiful speech in French about marriage and both my wife and the mouse cried.

After that there was no reason for Milliken to stay in Paris, and he moved back to the United States where he bought a house in Levittown, shaved off his beard, and got a job doing public relations for the Long Island Railroad. It's not a very pleasant picture and I try to drive it out of my mind. I always want to remember Milliken as the guy who almost broke the bank at Monte Carlo.

What's Happening in Paris

I'VE BEEN WONDERING how Americans have been faring in Paris since General de Gaulle broke with Britain over the Common Market. Several friends have smuggled out letters revealing that there have been many changes in the French attitude toward Americans, but it's hard to put a finger on all of them.

"The reason for this," one friend wrote me, "is that the French were never too friendly to Americans before, so it's hard to measure how unfriendly they are now. Then again, the French aren't too friendly to each other, so one is hard put to figure their new attitude toward us.

"I have noticed French school children saluting American officers with their left hands, if that means anything, and there seems to be a stepped-up drive to prevent Americans from finding decent parking places in Paris, but perhaps I'm being oversensitive.

"My concierge refuses to talk to me, but she never talked to me before de Gaulle came back to power, so I can't make a Federal case of that.

"The only overt act I have witnessed was in a restaurant the other night when two Americans walked in and the sommelier served them a bottle of Château d'Yquem with their fish course. Everyone knows you drink Château d'Yquem only with dessert. But the Americans had the good sense not to protest."

Another friend, Charles Torem, a lawyer, said he has been able to overcome the new anti-American feeling by doubling his tips. "I find I've had to tip twice as much as before and even so some taxi drivers still tell me they prefer de Gaulle to Kennedy."

Armin Roerrig, a student at the Sorbonne, says there have been noticeable changes in the attitudes toward him as an American since de Gaulle's famous press conference.

"I live with a French family, and ever since the Common Market talks broke off they've been taking a longer and longer time in the bathroom in the morning. Sometimes I don't get to shave until noon. Also, I find the radiator in my room apparently turned off every time I come home. And lately my landlady's daughter has taken to slamming the front door when she comes in late at night. This may be all part of a plot against me.

"At school the students have renounced chewing Wrigley's Spearmint and the coeds poke fun at Americans by calling each other 'baby doll' and 'sweetie pie.'"

One friend said he had noticed no changes in Paris until he went to the ice-skating rink at the Champs Elysées and noticed they were playing German music, including "The Ride of the Valkyries" from Richard Wagner's Ring Cycle, which caused the skaters to leap into the air in a very bellicose manner. In the bar he also noticed several young French boys making unpleasant noises on Coke bottles, signifying their disrespect for this most American of all drinks.

An American who travels on the Metro has discovered that if he wears an American emblem on his lapel and starts reading a copy of either *Time* magazine or *Newsweek*, no one will come near him. For the first time, he says, he has had breathing room in the subway.

I've received many more atrocity stories than I have room to report from Americans residing in Paris. But none can compare with a friend of mine who stopped in at the American Embassy in Paris and was informed by a French employee at one of the desks that according to the new United States law he would have to pay American income taxes. Fortunately for Franco-American relations, he managed to hold his temper.

Monaco Oui, France Non

THE NEWS OUT OF MONACO has shocked the free world. While American eyes have been diverted toward Cuba, General de Gaulle has put the squeeze on the tax-free people of the only absolute monarchy left in Europe. And yet, so far the American government has maintained a hands-off policy, and not one high official has come out to warn France that an attack on Monaco is an attack on the United States.

A French takeover of Monaco constitutes a direct threat to American interests in the Mediterranean. Monaco is only 3,645 miles off the coast of Florida. If the French take Monaco, they can set up a missile site (they can fit only one into the country) which could be aimed at the United States.

The French could use Monaco to blockade American Express bus tours. American collectors of Monaco stamps could be wiped out. American credit at the gambling casinos could be stopped arbitrarily. Post cards of Princess Grace, the only reigning American princess the United States has, could be banned.

But the State Department has sat on its hands and done nothing. Even the CIA, which seems to be in everything these days, has no plans for Monaco, except to fly a U-2 plane over it every other week.

Whenever there is a crisis, President Kennedy has asked authority to call up the reserves. Yet so far he hasn't asked for one extra man for Monaco.

And all you need to defend Monaco is one extra man.

To date Monaco has not become a political issue in the election campaigns, despite the fact that every American has a stake in the Riviera.

Prince Rainier, it is true, has made many mistakes. His most important one has been to keep the Communists out of his country. The United States will not come to the aid of any country that is not threatened by Communists. If he could prove that the Communists, instead of France, were trying to take over Monaco, we would have two United States Marine divisions there by morning. But since the threat comes from a Western country, Rainier has been left to fend for himself.

What Rainier needs right now are some Communists. A few years ago we reported that no European country would give up any of its Communists, for without Communists they would not be entitled to American aid. The only country willing to give up Communists is the United States. So if America would send several Communists to Monaco, we would then have the legal right to interfere there, since Monaco would then have a Communist threat which we couldn't sit by and do nothing about.

But since this might take some time (even in America Communists are hard to find), I think Rainier should take the following steps.

He should pretend that he has refused to allow a Negro student to attend the Monaco high school. This would give us a legitimate excuse to send Federal marshals to Monte Carlo to protect the student. Then, when it seems that they can't handle the situation, we would have to send in paratroopers to protect the marshals. Pretty soon we'd have Monaco ringed with troops and General de Gaulle would have second thoughts about taking over the principality.

If General de Gaulle still gave Prince Rainier a rough time, we could fine him $10,000 a day and deduct the money from foreign aid to France.

This is the only way we can help Prince Rainier and Princess Grace, without interfering in the internal affairs of their country.

Dream Interview with General de Gaulle

I HAD A DREAM interview with General Charles de Gaulle. Actually I intended to dream about interviewing Mr. Harold Macmillan, but every time I closed my eyes I saw General de Gaulle instead.

He was looking chipper when I met him. "Excuse me for being late," he said. "I was just taking a German lesson."

"Monsieur le Président, the Americans are very disturbed about your attitude toward Britain's entering the Common Market."

"What attitude?"

"Well, there is a feeling that you don't want Britain to join the Common Market."

"De Gaulle said that?"

"You're de Gaulle."

"I know who I am, thank you. It's all a frightful mistake. There is nothing I would rather see than the British in a united Europe. You see, it's very difficult for a small country like France to guide the destiny of something as complicated as the Common Market. If it were up to me, I would open up the Common Market to anyone in the world who wanted to join. But it's not up to me."

"Who is it up to?"

"De Gaulle."

"But you're de Gaulle," I said.

"I wish you wouldn't keep saying that. It's true I am de

Gaulle. But de Gaulle is France. And I can't very well speak for forty million Frenchmen, can I?"

"No, sir," I agreed. "Have you talked this over with de Gaulle?"

"Yes, but he's very stubborn about it. He feels the British aren't ready to be integrated into Europe. He's also mad because they accepted the Polaris missiles from the United States. He doesn't want to depend on the United States for his defense."

"But doesn't he feel that he will weaken the Western Alliance by becoming a third force?"

"Who feels that way?"

"De Gaulle."

"I'm de Gaulle. Who do you think you're talking to?"

"I wasn't sure. Anyway, what do you have to say about wrecking the Western Alliance?"

"De Gaulle feels you cannot wreck an alliance by developing your own atomic weapons. You in fact strengthen it. Suppose there is a situation where the United States does not want to use atomic missiles and we do. Well, if we have them, we can use them on our own, and there won't be any hard feelings between the United States and ourselves because they refused to let us have them. The only reason the Alliance is in jeopardy is because the United States has the weapons and we don't. Once we have the weapons we can only be friends."

"I never thought of that," I said. "There is a feeling among the other nations in the Common Market, though, that if Britain doesn't get in, France and Germany will dominate the continent."

"How could Germany dominate the continent if France intends to dominate it on its own?"

"Suppose West Germany wants atomic weapons in the near future?"

"Why should West Germany want atomic weapons, when we would have them to protect her? You can't give atomic weapons to every Ken, Nik, and Harold."

"Then what is your answer to the criticism about your attitude toward the Western Alliance?"

"Each nation in the West must search its soul and ask not what can de Gaulle do for it, but what can it do for de Gaulle."

It's Gaulling, But We'll Pay the Ransom

PRESIDENT CHARLES DE GAULLE'S press conference had many ominous overtones, and it has me worried sick. The usually good-natured, compromising head of state has suddenly turned on his friends and nobody knows what plans he has for the future relations between the United States and France.

After reading the text of the press conference, I became so worried that I immediately called up James B. Donovan, the lawyer, and asked him if he would be willing to negotiate a ransom settlement for the Americans who are still living in France. I explained to Donovan that while the matter wasn't pressing, I felt I should be prepared for the ransom demands which will probably come at the General's next press conference.

Donovan was very sympathetic and suggested I form a committee to liberate Americans in France. He felt I had some time to get organized as he didn't think the French would do anything until the *Mona Lisa* was returned to the Louvre.

Once the committee was formed and Bobby Kennedy gave me a tax-free status, Donovan said he would be willing to fly to Paris and talk to de Gaulle about terms.

"What do you think he'll want?" I asked him.

"We'll offer him pharmaceuticals, powdered milk, detergents, and a hundred hydrogen bombs."

"Do you think he'll be happy with that?"

"I don't think so, but we've got to start somewhere."

Donovan thought negotiations would be long and drawn out. "The trouble is most of the stuff we've got to offer de Gaulle is being produced by the Common Market and the ransom will be much higher than it was with Castro. Don't forget the Cuban ransom was only fifty-three million dollars. That will hardly buy you a meal at Maxim's these days."

"Suppose," I suggested, "we offer him fertilizer, tractors, the 101st Airborne Division, Cape Canaveral, and the ten best-dressed women of the year?"

"If Bobby agrees to it, I think it would be worth a try. But, remember, de Gaulle's in a very angry frame of mind. I think he'll want more than that."

"Well, why not throw in Detroit, the Metropolitan Museum of Art, two hundred Polaris submarines, and give him back Louisiana?"

"Okay," he said, "make up a list of the things you have to offer. We'll let the Red Cross check it, and then we'll submit it."

As soon as I hung up, I called Lucius Clay who said he'd raise any cash I needed. Then I hit a snag. Bobby Kennedy said Louisiana was not tax deductible, and neither were the ten best-dressed women of the year.

I substituted Mississippi and the New York newspaper printers' union instead. Pan American and TWA promised me that they would fly the Americans home once the ransom was paid.

The Government could not step in officially, but they said they would do everything they could to facilitate customs declarations.

And so we're all set. The committee to liberate Americans in France is prepared for the worst. Donovan is ready to fly to Paris as soon as I give him the word. We're not going to be caught short as we were at the Bay of Pigs. As soon as de Gaulle decides what he wants, he'll get it. After all he's done for us, that's the least we can do for him.

8.

WHEELINGS, DEALINGS, AND CEILINGS

My Old Kentucky Home, or
Oh, Ye Juleps and Colonels

TALK ABOUT NEWS MANAGEMENT, there are probably no newspapermen in the world managed like the ones who cover the Kentucky Derby. The first inkling of what was in store for me was when two men from the Old Fitzgerald Distillery (each distillery is assigned one newspaperman) met me at the ramp with a mint julep, a key to the city in the form of a bottle opener, and two choruses of "My Old Kentucky Home."

I was then placed in an automobile and driven to the Governor's Mansion in Frankfort, where I was given a mint julep and made an honorary Kentucky colonel. Then I went out on the lawn to hear the band play "My Old Kentucky Home."

An hour later I was back in Louisville. As I drove up to my Holiday Motel there was a large sign which read, "Welcome, Colonel Art Buchwald." I got out of the car and before anyone could stop me I sang "My Old Kentucky Home."

Two men from the Junior Chamber of Commerce were waiting for me in the lobby. They presented me with a mint julep, a colonel's hat, a colonel's tie, four cigars, and made me an honorary citizen of Louisville.

When I got to my room, cases of Old Fitzgerald were stacked in all the corners. Two bottles were placed on my pillow and there were several floating in the bathtub. I turned on the television set and they were singing "My Old Kentucky Home."

I mixed a mint julep and waited for something else to happen. It didn't take long. The two distillery men picked me up and took me to Churchill Downs where the Derby is run.

As I walked in the gate I was given a mint julep and over the loudspeaker I heard the strains of "My Old, Etc. Etc." I was taken to the press box and made an honorary member of the Churchill Downs Turf Writers' Brotherhood Week.

They let me make a bet on a horse and then I was made an honorary member of the Turf Writers' Losers Association.

Someone handed me a mint julep and I bet it on the next race. I won and the mint julep paid 5 to 1. I was getting a little dizzy.

The two distillery men asked me if I would appear on television, which was being shot from the race track, and I said I would. So they made me an honorary television guest, and I told them all about the difference between racing at Ascot and racing at Churchill Downs.

"The main difference," I mumbled, "is that at Ascot they don't make the mint juleps so strong."

I thought after the television show I would be finished for the day but, of course, I was mistaken.

One of the distillery men said, "It is our job to see you have a good time."

I started to sing "My Old Kentucky Home."

"No, wait. We have an honor for you that is rarely bestowed on anyone that visits Louisville."

"You're going to make me an honorary mint julep," I said, swaying slightly.

"No, it's even more important than that."

"So, tell me," I said, holding onto the rail as the track started to move up and down.

"We're going to make you an honorary horse."

The One-Hundred-Dollar Bet

WELL, THE EIGHTY-NINTH running of the Kentucky Derby is over, but the memory lingers on. I think of all the memories, the one I'll remember the most was losing one hundred dollars on my boss's hoss No Robbery.

Don't get me wrong. I wasn't apple-polishing when I bet on the boss's hoss. I believed in my heart of hearts No Robbery was going to be the winner, and I plunged deep into my pocket to back him.

Well, the boss's hoss lost and now I have to explain the loss to the hoss's boss. How do I do it?

"Mr. Whitney, as you know, the price of mint juleps has gone up in Louisville. . . ."

No, he would never buy that. Perhaps the light touch.

"Mr. Whitney, a funny thing happened to me on the way home from the race track. . . ."

But would he think it was very funny?

"Mr. Whitney, I took Chateaugay, the winner of the Derby, out to dinner Saturday night, and you'll never believe this but he ate a hundred dollars in oats."

Why should Mr. Whitney entertain another horse? After all, Chateaugay won $105,000.

"Mr. Whitney, I know you won't believe this, but I took a taxi to Churchill Downs Saturday and we got lost and the meter read one hundred dollars. Kentucky cabdrivers are worse than those in Paris."

Frankness, that's what I should use.

"Mr. Whitney, I'd like to talk to you as a friend and not an employee. . . ."

Hmmm. That's not bad.

Or, maybe, "Mr. Whitney, I'd like to talk to you as an employee and not a friend."

That sounds sincere and has the right touch.

"Mr. Whitney, I spent a hundred dollars in Louisville and I just can't seem to account for it."

It's reasonable. Anyone can spend a hundred dollars and not account for it.

But perhaps I should be more conniving.

"Mr. Whitney, do you know they have pickpockets at the Kentucky Derby? I think we should have an editorial about it. How much did I get my pocket picked for? One hundred dollars. That's how much. Oh, no, I refuse to accept. After all, it was my pocket. I don't see why you should be responsible."

There must be a better way than that.

"Mr. Whitney, I know the strike was very costly. But I was wondering if you would be willing to contribute one hundred dollars to the Syndicated Columnists' Widows and Orphans Fund?

But suppose he gave me the money and then tried to deduct it from his income tax? Then I'd really be in a mess.

"Mr. Whitney, I know you're wondering why I put down one hundred dollars on my expense account as 'miscellaneous.' Well, it's a long story and I'd rather not bore you with the details. . . . What's that, you don't mind being bored? . . . I mean, we . . . it was Derby day and this fellow offered to let me sit in the Governor's box for only ten dollars and I thought this would be a wonderful way to see the race. Well, I bought the ticket and when I got to the box I discovered it was for the 1962 Derby. So the State troopers took me down to headquarters and I was fined ninety dollars for accusing the Governor of taking my seat."

It was strong, but maybe it was too strong.

There must be a way.

Truth. Mr. Whitney always admires someone who tells the truth.

"Hello, Mr. Whitney. Sorry to bother you about a petty matter, but last Saturday I bet a hundred dollars on your horse No Robbery . . . hello, Mr. Whitney—Mr. Whitney— Operator, operator, I've been cut off."

Touting the Soviet Envoy

I WENT TO LAUREL PARK for the running of the famed Washington, D. C., International horse race which the French horse Match II won in a thrilling finish. I happened to be the guest of John Schapiro, owner of the track, who has a

private turf club of his own where one hundred distinguished members of the diplomatic corps, horse owners,
and trainers drank champagne while they watched the
festivities.

As luck would have it, I was seated next to the Soviet
ambassador to the United States, Anatoly Dobrynin, who
was witnessing his first American horse race. Russia had two
horses in the International, so Ambassador Dobrynin had a
very legitimate reason for being there.

I nervously avoided discussing politics, figuring if the
ambassador had anything to tell me he would, and talked
about horses instead, a subject which neither one of us knew
anything about.

Just before the third race I asked him if I could place a
bet for him.

"Yes," he said, "you choose a horse and bet it for me."

"Don't you want to choose your own horse?" I asked him.

"No," he said, "I trust you."

I left the table perspiring. No one in the history of horse
racing had been given a responsibility like this! If I picked a
loser, relations between the Soviet Union and the United
States might get worse. But if I picked a winner, this might
give the ambassador confidence, which is certainly something
I didn't want him to have at the time.

I tried to call Arthur Schlesinger for guidance, but he wasn't
in. I then called the National Security Council, but they were
in session and couldn't be disturbed.

Walter Lippmann was out of town, Joseph Alsop was taking
a nap. There was no one I could ask for help.

Finally I went to Mr. Schapiro and told him the problem.
"Do we want the Soviet ambassador to have a winner at this
stage in the negotiations?" I asked him.

"I think we'd better," he said. "Bet four dollars for him on
Potato Chip."

I bet the four dollars and sure enough Potato Chip won
over Sun Shiner.

The ambassador was elated as Potato Chip paid twenty

dollars for four dollars. His spirits were high, and I was sure the Russian bombers would be out of Cuba by morning.

But then the "OBJECTION" light went up. Sun Shiner claimed a foul against Potato Chip. I sat there nervously as the foul was disputed. All sorts of thoughts ran through my head. Maybe the CIA had heard about it and wanted the Russian ambassador to lose. Perhaps a John Bircher had got control of the tote board. Maybe the Russians had stuck a missile under Potato Chip's saddle. But fortunately the judges discounted the foul claim and Potato Chip was declared the winner.

I breathed easier. The ambassador insisted I bet the next race for him. I sought out Mr. Schapiro again. "He wants another winner."

"Bet Joe Cave," Mr. Schapiro said.

Joe Cave came in fourth. Maybe the bombers would stay.

In the fifth race Mr. Schapiro gave us King's Idyll, who also ran out of the money. I hated to face the ambassador. But when I got back to the table he was called to the phone. He rushed back and said, "Excuse me, I have to leave immediately."

"Aren't you staying for the big race?" I asked.

"No, I must leave right now."

"But, I'll find you another winner," I said.

"Please excuse me. It's very important," and he dashed away.

I went up to Schapiro. "What do you make of it?" I asked him.

"It might have something to do with Cuba; it might have something to do with China; or it might have something to do with those last two losers."

"Maybe we ought to head for the hills," I said to Mr. Schapiro. "We can listen to the big race on a transistor radio."

"No, I'll have to stick it out here," he said. "If it's a false alarm I'd never forgive myself."

"You do what you want, but I'm going to find myself a cave. Nobody leaves before a big race unless it means—"

"Don't say it," Mr. Schapiro said.

And I didn't. But it taught me a lesson. In times like these even a race track isn't a safe place to be.

Baseball à la Grecque

THE GAME OF BASEBALL can be Greek to a lot of people, particularly if you are Greek. I had the pleasure of watching a world series game on television with Melina Mercouri, the Greek actress who was in Washington with her director, Jules Dassin, promoting their film, *Phaedra*. Miss Mercouri didn't want to watch the game, but Mr. Dassin had his heart set on it.

"Darling," he said, "this is the world series. I've got to see it."

"What countries are playing?" Miss Mercouri wanted to know.

"No countries are playing. It is between two American teams."

"Then why do they call it the world series?" she asked.

"I guess because to Americans it is the most important thing in the world. You see, baseball is the national pastime."

"In Greece we have better pastimes," the actress said.

"Yes," Mr. Dassin agreed, "but you can't show them on television."

"I don't care, I want to see the White House and the Capitol and the Pentagon. I don't want to sit in this hotel room looking at a stupid game."

"It's not stupid. Let me explain it to you. Look at the screen. There are nine men on each team."

"Who is the man in the blue suit with the life preserver?" Miss Mercouri wanted to know.

"That's the umpire. He's neutral."

"I like him. He's dressed much better than the others."

"Now pay attention," Mr. Dassin said. "There are four bases, including home plate. The man with the bat stands at home plate and tries to hit the ball which is thrown by a man called the pitcher."

"And the rest of them just stand around doing nothing," Miss Mercouri said.

"No, that's not so. If the man hits the ball, they must try to catch it and put him out."

"That's all they do?"

"Well, they also have to bat when it is their turn. Now watch, the pitcher has just thrown a ball."

"The man didn't try to hit the ball," Miss Mercouri said.

"No, he didn't, because the pitch was a ball."

"I know it was a ball. I can see."

"You don't understand. It was a bad ball."

"Why don't they play with good balls? I thought America was a rich country."

"They do play with good balls. But if the ball doesn't go over the plate it's called a ball. Now look, he just hit a foul ball. That's a strike."

Miss Mercouri looked at Mr. Dassin incredulously. "A bad ball is a ball, and a foul ball is a strike? Why isn't a bad ball a foul ball? Tell me, who is on strike?"

"Nobody is on strike," Mr. Dassin said. "It's called a strike. Watch, you see, the man just hit a fly to center field."

"You saw a man hit a fly on television?" Miss Mercouri asked.

"Not a real fly. It's called a fly if it goes in the air."

"I want to see the Supreme Court," Miss Mercouri said.

"Wait a minute. The next batter is the best player on the team. Let's see what he does. Look, he just made a long drive into center field and he has a double."

"A double what?"

"Just a double. He has two bases."

"I don't see them," Miss Mercouri said.

"It's two up and two down and a man on second."

"Who's up and who's down?"

"Never mind. If they get one more out, they'll retire the side."

"Can we go sight-seeing if they retire the side?"

"No, because then the other team is up at bat."

"It's a stupid game," Miss Mercouri said.

Mr. Dassin was getting desperate. Suddenly he thought of something. "Do you know, the best hitter on the Yankees is a Greek?"

For the first time Miss Mercouri took an interest in the game. "What's his name?"

"Mickey Mantoupoplous. They call him Mickey Mantle for short."

"Come on, Mickey Mantoupoplous," Miss Mercouri shouted. "Hit the foul ball over the home plate and show them you can double the bases with two up and two down and don't forget to retire to the side!"

"That's it," Mr. Dassin said. "You're getting the hang of it. Now, isn't this better than sight-seeing?"

"Are there any Greeks on the other side?" Miss Mercouri wanted to know.

"Just Willie Mays," Mr. Dassin said, "Just Willie Mays."

Grown-up League Baseball

A LOT HAS BEEN WRITTEN about Little League baseball, but a new craze has hit the American scene which could be called Grown-up League baseball. What apparently happened was that parents, after watching their kids play baseball for so long, got bored and suddenly decided they wanted to play the game themselves. So now, all across the country on Sunday afternoons, parents are stealing their kids' gloves, bats, and baseballs, and are sneaking off to the nearest playground to have a game.

Some kids have protested this infringement on the sport, particularly when they're left at home to mow the lawn or water the plants, but other kids have got into the spirit of the thing and have volunteered their services as coaches, umpires, and trainers. As one boy put it, "It keeps our parents off the streets, and at least we know where they are."

One Sunday I attended a Grown-up League game at the Phoebe Hearst playground in northwest Washington. My nine-year-old son caught me stealing his glove, so he demanded the right to come along. Since we had only one glove between us, I insisted that as his father I had the right to play.

"Well, what am I going to do?" he protested.

"Why don't you go behind a bush and smoke a cigarette?"

"I did it last week," he said. "It makes me sick."

"Here are some rocks. Go over and break the school windows."

"That's no fun. I want to play baseball."

"You should be ashamed of yourself," I told him. "You know what happens to kids who play baseball?"

"What?" he asked.

"They grow up and bet on games and get fined by the baseball commissioner."

"That's football," he said.

I was still struggling for the glove.

"Please let me play," I begged. "I've got so few years left for the game. Someday, when you grow up and become a father, you'll know what it means to want to play baseball."

"Well, what am I going to do?" he demanded.

"Hang around a drugstore like other kids. How do I know what to do? Look at the other fathers. Are their kids giving them a bad time about playing?"

I saw three fathers also struggling for baseball gloves, and one mother pleading with her son to let her have the bat.

Finally, we compromised. If my son let me play baseball on Sunday, he could play poker at the National Press Club the following Saturday night.

About thirty-two parents showed up to play, so the captains, not wanting to hurt anyone's feelings, chose sixteen players for each side. The infield was so crowded that it looked like a student demonstration in Caracas. But despite the size of the teams, everyone seemed to have a good time and got to bat at least once.

Once my son got over his disappointment at not playing, he was very helpful. After I flied out to third base, he said, "You have to loosen up, Dad, and don't choke up on your bat so much."

When my team lost the game, my son was right there to comfort me as I wept unashamedly.

"You played your best," he said as he gave me a cold can of beer. "Here, drink this and you'll feel better. After all, it's only a game."

La Dolce Vita, *Air-line Style*

I FOLLOWED the congressional hearings on alleged air-line violations with interest. Several stewardesses testified that they had flown passenger planes, and one young lady had seen another stewardess sitting on the lap of the chief pilot while the plane was in flight.

This bears out a story I heard some time ago when a friend of mine was taking a flight. The captain's voice came over the loudspeaker, "This is your pilot, Captain Zilch. We will be flying at 18,000 feet at a speed of 450 miles an hour," and so on. The captain thought his microphone was cut off and he said to his copilot, "Boy, could I use a cup of coffee and a stewardess sitting in my lap right now." Unfortunately, everyone on the plane heard him and the stewardess ran down the aisle to warn the captain his microphone was still on. But as she passed my friend, he shouted at her, "Hey, you forgot the coffee."

True or not, the revelation that stewardesses have been flying planes and that pilots have been having a ball at the controls makes flying even more interesting than it had been before.

I can just imagine a flight if it was as described in the testimony.

"Good evening, ladies and gentlemen, this is your stewardess, Ann McGarry. Tonight we will be flying at—oops—stop it, Fred, until I get the announcement over with—at 30,000 feet. Just a little ice, dear, and plenty of water. Your pilot, who is sitting just below me, is Captain— Fred, honey, what did you say your last name was? Sparkle? Fred Sparkle. And your copilot— Jean, what's your date's name? Jean, come up for air! What's your fellow's name? Harry? Harry Airelon.

"Your other stewardess is Jean Throttleall, and she will be your navigator. During your flight your captain and copilot will be glad to serve you coffee and sandwiches. I will be taking off in a few minutes as soon as we get more ice cubes. Hush, Fred, I'm talking to the passengers. What's that? You want to say something to the passengers?"

"Shut up and deal."

The stewardess comes back on the mike. "Let's see, where were we? I think we're ready to take off. Please fasten your safety belts. And—did anybody bring any cigarettes?"

"I got some, but they're filtered."

"It doesn't make any difference. Gee, this is an uncomfortable position."

"Well, if you're going to fly the plane, you're going to have to sit in my lap. The regulations say the pilot must remain in his seat at all times."

"Well, why don't you fly the plane, then?"

"Because you're the stewardess. I already know how to fly it. You have to learn sometime."

"All right, I'll fly it just this once, but you're going to have to land it."

"Gee, honey, the night's still young. No use talking about landing already."

"Now don't get fresh. I'm not one of those stewardesses who, just because the pilot lets me sit in his lap, will let him take liberties with me."

"Of course you're not. If you were, I wouldn't let you fly the plane."

"Well, I guess we better get started. And don't mess up my make-up until I put us on automatic pilot."

Too Old To Fly

THERE HAS BEEN A CONTROVERSY among the air lines over the age at which stewardesses should be grounded. American Airlines decided that when a girl reaches her thirty-second birthday she should no longer be allowed to fly.

Naturally the stewardesses, particularly those approaching that age limit, complained. But American stuck by its guns, or whatever an air line sticks by, and said that at thirty-two a stewardess should be ready to take a job on the ground.

My sympathies happen to be with the older stewardesses on this matter. Perhaps it's because, having lived in Europe for such a long period of time, I know that a woman doesn't even blossom until she reaches the age of thirty-two.

The Europeans think of their women differently than the Americans do. In America everything is slanted toward youth. In Europe the chic woman, the attractive woman, the woman that really matters, is aged anywhere from thirty to fifty. Sure, Europeans may ogle a Lolita of twenty-four or twenty-five, and we even know of cases of Frenchmen dating girls as young as twenty-one. But when it comes to any serious business such as flying, Europeans want their women beautiful but mature.

Besides, there are many of us who are afraid to fly, and have a mother fixation when we get in the air.

I've been doing quite a bit of flying in the United States, and I always feel safer with an older hostess just as I do with an older pilot. A young stewardess doesn't seem as interested in your problems. She doesn't show the compassion for you that a thirty-two-year-old stewardess does. You can talk to an older stewardess, tell her about your troubles at home, how bad your work is going, how you hate to fly. When the trip gets bumpy you can put your head in her lap and she'll comfort you. All the younger stewardesses ever think about is if you have enough coffee in your cup, or if you have something to read.

Younger stewardesses also have a tendency to upset the passengers. Many times I've witnessed wives becoming furious at their husbands because the husbands were watching a pretty young thing in uniform strut down the aisle. I've also seen grown men upset trays of food, just because some young hostess leaned over to adjust their safety belts. But nothing happens with the older, more mature hostesses. They have the air of a professional nurse about them. Your eyes don't have to stray from your magazine every time they walk by. You can keep your thoughts on where you're going and what you're going to do.

And one more thing. Older hostesses know how to cook better. Have you ever compared a meal prepared on board a plane by a twenty-one-year-old hostess with one prepared by a thirty-two-year-old hostess?

There is just no comparison.

There are many of us flying today who not interested in looking at a young, pretty, sexy girl in uniform. We believe in chic older women in their thirties.

I sincerely hope American Airlines reconsiders its policy almost as much as I hope my wife reads this.

Collect Call from Las Vegas

THERE COMES A TIME in every man's life when, if he is in Las Vegas alone, he has to call his wife—collect. The moment came earlier for me than I expected, and the call went something like this.

"Hello, dear," I said. "I'm calling from Las Vegas."

"I know where you're calling from," she said, the bitterness seeping through the receiver. "What did you do last night?"

"I had a date with a show girl," I told her.

"Don't lie to me. You were gambling."

"Just a little. Nothing much."

"How much did you lose?"

"I love you," I told her.

"I said how much did you lose?"

"I didn't call to talk about that. I called to talk about the children."

"What about the children?" she wanted to know.

"Why do they have to go to college when they grow up? Lots of children don't go to college and turn out to be wonderful parents."

"You didn't lose their college money?" she screamed.

"Only their junior and senior years."

"What else did you lose?"

"Where are you standing now?"

"In our bedroom," she replied.

"Please don't say 'our' bedroom any more."

"You didn't lose the house?" she asked incredulously.

"Just parts of it. I kept title to the basement and the garage."

I could hear sobbing on the other end of the line.

"Now, wait a minute, dear. You said the house was too big for us anyway and you would prefer something smaller. Think of it as a lucky break. Dear, are you there?"

"Yes, I'm here."

"Do me a favor. You know that gold necklace with the pearls I bought you for our anniversary?"

"You lost that?"

"Of course not. Do you think I would do something that low?"

"Well, what about the necklace?"

"I want you to go out and lose it somewhere so we can collect the insurance on it. We'll get a much better price than if we try to sell it."

"I could kill you," she said.

"Don't. It would be a mistake."

"You mean you lost your life insurance, too?"

"They told me a man who plays the way I do will live forever."

"Well, at least you didn't lose my fur coat."

I didn't say anything.

"You *did* lose my fur coat?"

"Who wears a fur coat in Washington?" I replied.

"When are you coming home?"

"That's what I called about. There's a Greyhound bus leaving for Washington at three this afternoon, and if you send me the money I left you for food I'll be on it."

"And what are we going to eat until you get here?"

"Call up the Department of Agriculture. According to the law we're entitled to participate in their surplus food program."

Gin Rummy Tournament

"LAS VEGAS," a friend told me, "is the only city in the world where they hang banners in the streets saying 'Welcome Gin Rummy Players.'"

The occasion for the banners was the Seventh International Gin Rummy Tournament, which was held here under the auspices of the Las Vegas Charities organization. As an *aficionado* of the second greatest American indoor sport (the first one is beating your kids) I was delighted to attend as a spectator and part-time competitor.

It's hard to believe, but there are 34,896,455 gin rummy players in the United States of America today, of which only 34,896,453 are fanatical about the game. The other two play it "because it's there."

Although gin is played for money and the stakes can be as little as a quarter of a cent a point up to two dollars a point, it was recently ruled not a game of chance, but one of skill. This came about when police raided the Regency Bridge

Club in Santa Monica, and several gin players were arrested for gambling on the premises. Judge Henry H. Drager, who had played gin rummy in his youth, ruled after hearing exhaustive testimony that gin was as much a game of skill as bridge. In the eyes of players everywhere he has become gin rummy's own Oliver Wendell Holmes.

But back to the tournament—804 men and women from every State in the Union showed up to compete for the $35,000 in prizes. Anyone with one hundred dollars could enter the competition and while every gin rummy player cannot be a winner, every gin rummy player considers himself a champion. Therefore you had 804 champions playing against each other in hotel ballrooms all over town.

By the time I arrived, it was too late to play in the tournament, but as a consolation the organizers let me play a grandmother from Pasadena, who had been eliminated in the semifinals when her opponent, taking advantage of the woman's bad eyesight, knocked with two points while the poor old lady was waiting for a third king.

The grandmother, who looked like a cross between "Whistler's Mother" and the little old lady in Ernest Hemingway's *Death in the Afternoon,* was a relentless opponent. She knocked on the third card, undercut me four times, and blitzed me once. (You are blitzed when you don't score any points.)

Just when I was recovering and had her on the run, I broke a fingernail and lost all control of the game. Since I couldn't hold my cards neatly, I went down to defeat with the sound of the grandmother's chortles in my ears. (Gin rummy winners either laugh, smile, or chortle, depending on the score.)

But it was my own fault. If I had thrown an eight of diamonds instead of a four of hearts, and she had given me the ten of clubs, which she didn't need anyway, I would have discarded the three of spades, which would have forced her to knock with three when I had two and the whole picture of the game would have been different. Ask any gin player and he'll tell you the exact same thing.

New Transportation Worth
a Lusty Toot

A FELLOW CAME INTO the office and asked, "How would you like to take a new type train to Miami, Florida?"

"What's a train?" I asked him.

"Well, it looks like a series of buses hooked up together and the wheels placed on these steel rails and it's pulled along by an engine."

"That's the silliest thing I've ever heard," I said. "Is it safe?"

"Some people," he said, "think it's safer than flying. You may not believe this, but trains were invented before planes."

"Now you're pulling my leg," I said angrily. "Why don't people use them if they're that good?"

"People used to use them to go to Florida, but planes are so much faster. At the same time you see things on a train, and you can sleep and relax and play cards and walk around. We on the Atlantic Coast Line think trains are coming back and so we've put on this special train with stewardesses and motion pictures and bingo and community singing and fashion shows, and this way we think people will enjoy taking the train. We in the railroad business believe that if God wanted people to fly he would have given them wings."

Well, I had nothing to do and I was curious to see what a train looked like, so I took the trip to Miami. It certainly looked strange at first, but once I was assured the train couldn't go off the rails I relaxed and started to enjoy myself.

I was given a compartment all to myself which isn't too much fun if you don't like being alone, so I went forward to the club car where I met the stewardess, a very attractive young lady who used to sing in the choir of a Presbyterian church.

"Would you like to play bingo?" the stewardess asked.

"I didn't come here to see *Hamlet*," I told her, and then after we both laughed, she gave me a card.

We played bingo for about an hour, and each time someone won he received a bottle of sun-tan lotion. Well, after everyone won a bottle of sun-tan lotion, the stewardess asked who would like to sing and we all raised our hands, so everyone was given a song sheet and we started singing "Dixie," "Old Black Joe," "Oh, Susanna," and "Deep in the Heart of Texas."

About an hour and a half later they showed us some movies of Florida, and then they let us go eat. After dinner we had free time, but none of us knew what to do with it, so we started singing some more. Then we all went off to bed.

One thing trains had over planes, our guide said, was that weather couldn't stop a train as it did a plane and at least you knew you were arriving on time. I said there was something in that. But then we got outside of Fort Lauderdale and the train came to a halt. A drawbridge wouldn't go down and we got stuck there.

But it didn't spoil my trip. You don't get bingo and community singing on airplanes these days, and besides, on a train there is no possible way of the stewardess's getting up to the engineer's cockpit. This is a factor that someone traveling these days should not take lightly.

Bullfights and Marriage

EVERYONE READS something different into a bullfight. Usually bullfighting is associated with death, but I went to a fight in Dax with a recently divorced friend who insisted bullfighting has more to do with marriage than anything else.

"To me," he said, "it is the complete drama of wedlock."

"How's that?" I asked him.

"Let us start at the beginning. Before us we see the beautifully dressed matador—he represents the bride, slim, confident, completely in charge of the situation. Now look, the bull has just come into the ring. He is the groom. He is magnificent but bewildered, confused, and sorry he is there. The crowd is cheering. Why? Because it is a wedding day, and people always cheer at weddings.

"Now the bull is snorting and charging, but the matador waves the cape. She is playing with him, making him think he has the upper hand, but what the matador is really doing is finding out the bull's weaknesses, and also making him use up all his energy."

"What's happening now?" I asked him, trying to look at the bullfight through his eyes.

"The trumpets have sounded, the wedding ceremony is over, and now the marriage begins in earnest. First come the picadors; they represent the wife's relatives. The bull is furious, but the picadors keep stabbing him in the neck and shoulders and pretty soon the bull can hardly lift his eyes."

"I see what you're driving at," I said.

"Now come the banderilleros, who represent the wife's friends. They also are there to weaken the bull's muscles, and make him bleed some more. By this time he can't keep his head up.

"This is the final act. Watch carefully. The matador, or wife, is no longer playing with the bull. Now she is serious. She holds out the red cloth, and like a fool the bull makes a pass at it. Then he makes another. He never charges the matador, only the cloth. The bull doesn't know it, but he is wearing himself out. He's in pretty desperate condition, anyway, after what the relatives and friends have done to him. But he is angry and this is a last gasp on his part. The more the matador makes a fool of the bull, the more the crowd cheers. The crowd is aways on the side of the wife."

"Just like in real life," I said.

"We are ready for the moment of truth. The bull, hurt, bewildered, and tired, looks at the matador. The matador stands in front of him and now—she plunges the sword deep into his heart. The bull staggers for several minutes in shock and then collapses. The marriage is finished and the matador, or wife, is presented with the bull's ears and tail, which she holds up in the ring to show everyone."

"What do the ears and tail represent?" I asked my friend.

He looked at me with the saddest eyes I had ever seen and replied, "Alimony."

Bucket-seat Trauma

THE AUTOMOBILE MANUFACTURERS have done it again. They've got the college kids furious at them over one of the most insidious features of the 1963 car—the bucket seat.

The bucket seat, originally put in sports cars with a console dividing the driver and his partner, has now become standard optional equipment on most of the conventional models. It provides for only two seats in the front, and they're separated. The college students feel the automobile companies have ganged up on them and have taken the togetherness out of the American educational system.

Among the most disappointed are the students at the University of Detroit, who feel that since Detroit is the automobile capital of the United States, they should have been consulted by the designers before the bucket seats were installed.

I was in Detroit to give a lecture, and so I went out to the school and attended an informal seminar of Detroit University students concerning the problem. Jim Fiebig, who works on the *Varsity News,* has a theory that a lady spinster reached all the automobile companies and persuaded them to install the bucket seat. "She must be found," he cried, "she must be eliminated."

A young lady at the seminar told of a frightening experience she had had in a Thunderbird, one of the first cars to install the bucket seat. "We went on this date and we parked, and then we just sat there. My date reached over to put his arm around my shouder and he could just barely touch the arm closest to him.

"Finally he took off his sports jacket and rolled it up and placed it on the console between us. But I'm five-foot-five and when I sat on his jacket my head hit the roof. I was towering over him, and he didn't like that, so he drove me home in disgust. I haven't seen him since. And it wasn't my fault."

Another student said he thought the bucket seat was un-American and was driving a wedge between parents and their offspring. "Who wants to borrow his father's car if it has bucket seats?" he said. "Maybe parents will buy them just so we won't ask."

"The trouble with bucket seats," a young lady said, "is when you ride in them, everyone thinks you're married. Why else would you sit so far away from the driver?"

One student, who was roundly booed, said, "I think bucket seats are okay. Women are getting too aggressive these days, anyway."

A girl interjected. "The only time they're any good is if you don't like the guy you're going out with. Then you have a perfect excuse to stay where you are."

"It's a plot by the manufacturers of Indian blankets," a student shouted. "I wouldn't be surprised if Henry Ford owned part of a blanket company."

"The bucket seat presents many problems for a woman," a pretty coed said. "For one thing they're very difficult to get into, but worse still, they're more difficult to get out of."

One student had a solution. "I think if the automobile manufacturers are going to sell cars with bucket seats, they should send demonstrators around with them. They should hire some unfrocked pilots to show us how *they* managed to neck in the bucket seats of their airplanes. I mean with lessons maybe we could get used to the new cars."

"Do you think," suggested another student, "that bucket seats were put in by President Kennedy to further his physical fitness program for youth?"

"Maybe," replied a young man. "He is always saying he wants the country to keep moving."

"Well, I'll tell you one thing," a coed said. "Bucket seats

are going to put the drive-in movie theaters out of business. Who wants to go to a drive-in and see the movies they're making these days?"

Mr. Fiebig revealed he had taken a girl to a drive-in with a borrowed bucket-seat car and when she leaned toward him to turn up the speaker she disappeared. He found her after the picture was over, between the seats, groaning piteously with a broken sacroiliac.

9.

SOUTHERN EXPOSURE

A Class at Ole Miss

ONE CAN'T HELP WONDERING what they're teaching down at Ole Miss during all the trouble there. I can only speculate as to what is going on in the classrooms. How, for example, do they teach the United States Constitution? Perhaps something like this.

The professor speaks. "Now, class, today we're going to discuss the American Constitution, a very unique document, which, while it has nothing to do with us, should be studied anyway to show how other people govern themselves.

"The most interesting part of the Constitution is the preamble, which begins, 'They, the people of the United States, in order to form a more perfect union—' "

A student stands up. "Sir, do the people of the *United States* really believe in the Constitution?"

"Now, let's not be too harsh on them. It is a primitive document with many flaws in it, but there are also some good things in it, and even we in Mississippi have taken some things from the American Constitution to govern ourselves. For example, there is the freedom of speech amendment. Now, this is a very good thing. We also believe in freedom of speech, and we have never stopped anyone in Mississippi from yelling 'Help!' if he so desired.

"Freedom of religion is another thing we've taken from the United States Constitution. We not only encourage them to pray—we make them. We encourage prayer as a way of solving problems that other States solve in the law courts. As a matter of fact, if a sociological problem can't be solved by prayer, then we believe there is no reason to solve it.

"The Second Amendment of the United States Constitution also has some merit—the right to keep and bear arms. As our greatest constitutional expert, Major General Edwin A. Walker, has pointed out, every citizen has the right to bear arms against the United States. Otherwise, what kind of a government could you possibly have?"

A student raises his hand. "Do we go along with the Sixth Amendment, which provides the right to a speedy trial?"

"Yes, we do," the professor replies. "If anyone in Mississippi whom we don't like tries to register to vote, he is entitled to a speedy trial."

Another student raises his hand. "What about the right to petition and the right to peacefully assemble?"

The professor replies, "We believe in them and proof of it is that we have permitted people to petition and to assemble to prevent Mr. Meredith from enrolling in our university."

A student raises his hand. "The Americans have an Amendment which says that excessive bail shall not be required, nor excessive fines imposed, nor cruel and unusual punishments inflicted. Is this a good thing?"

"Well, that's what they believe in and who is to say under their system whether it's wrong or right? You must understand that what is constitutional in one part of the country doesn't necessarily make it constitutional in another. Otherwise our Governor would be in court all the time."

A student stands. "Amendment Fifteen says the right of citizens to vote shall not be denied or abridged by the United States or any State on account of race, color, or previous condition of servitude. How are we to take this Amendment?"

The professor says, "I didn't understand the question."

The student starts to ask the question again and the professor pushes a button on his desk. Two State highway patrolmen come into the classroom and drag the student out.

As the class settles down, the professor says, "If there is anything I hate worse than a Negro, it's a Constitution-lover."

François Writes to Pierre

My CHER PIERRE,

Please forgive me for not writing sooner, but I've just been down at the University of Mississippi lecturing to the students on the French constitution and the ways General de Gaulle ignores it. They were most interested in the fact that the Government had just fallen in France, and were wondering how they could make the Government fall in the United States.

I explained to them that under their Constitution it was very difficult to dissolve the Government, because, if the President resigned, the job would automatically go to one of his brothers. Under the French system, if General de Gaulle resigned, he would automatically succeed himself.

I must say the students were a lively group and asked me countless questions, such as: "What were the best methods you used in keeping the Algerians from voting?" "What were the ingredients that went into the making of plastic bombs?" "How much would it cost to ship the French Foreign Legion to Mississippi?" and "Would General Salan consider taking over the governorship of their sovereign State?"

The students also wanted to know if the Sorbonne in Paris had integrated education. When I told them it had, they wept. "Even in Paris," one student said. "Isn't there any place left where we can study in peace?"

But I cheered them up by showing them films of the barricades the French citizens had built in Paris during one of the last demonstrations. They were most interested in our cobblestone streets and many came to the conclusion that, if they had had cobblestones in Oxford, they would have won the day.

They were so pleased with my talk they gave me a souvenir gas mask that they had stolen from a Federal marshal the night before.

You asked me in your last letter what the Americans were talking about. For the moment you hear nothing but talk about Cuba. It seems that the Americans have just discovered that Cuba is only ninety miles from the United States. It's been ninety miles from the United States for years, but nobody bothered to measure it until recently. Now that the Americans have discovered it's such a short distance, they want to attack it.

The Americans are very upset because Russia has been supplying Cuba with arms and technicians and therefore it's become a Communist threat in this hemisphere. But the issue has become clouded because former Vice-President Nixon, who is running for Governor of California, says there is a Communist threat in California, which his opponent, Governor Brown, has done nothing about. Now California is less than ninety miles away from the United States, and therefore some hotheads want to blockade California instead of Cuba.

Congress has just passed a "Fight If We Must" resolution which gives the President an opportunity to attack Cuba at his own discretion. I have pointed out to my friends that when France and Great Britain wanted to attack Suez because their interests were endangered there, the United States stopped us and said we were violating the UN Charter.

"Yes," they said, "but that's because you didn't have the Monroe Doctrine."

How could I argue with that?

Your cher ami,
François

The Communists Are Pleased

THE EVENTS IN BIRMINGHAM have people talking everywhere. While they haven't caused much joy in the United States, they have brought happiness to many parts of the world, particularly Moscow.

I can just imagine what is going on now in one of the long corridors of the Kremlin.

"Ah, Comrade Milichef, your people have done a wonderful job in Alabama."

"My people? I am afraid you are mistaken. My department had nothing to do with it. I thought your department arranged it, Comrade Zuchovitch."

"I wish it was so. From a propaganda viewpoint it is one of the biggest victories we've had this year. The Chairman is terribly pleased. Our embassies in Asia and Africa report that the photos have been on the front pages of the local newspapers and Birmingham is now a household name."

"But if it wasn't your department and it wasn't my department, who could have arranged it?"

"Perhaps Rokosky. He once suggested using police dogs on children in East Germany. His people may have infiltrated the Birmingham police department."

"I thought of that. But you know what a blow-hard Rokosky is. If his people had done it he would run up and down the corridors telling everyone."

"What about Poslov? Wasn't it Poslov who perfected the fire-hose offensive in Poland?"

"But that wasn't the real stroke of genius. It was locking up the children in jail. Somebody from our side must have persuaded the police chief that this was the thing to do."

"I can't believe they would be that stupid. We must have someone very high in the government helping us."

"Who would it be?"

"The Governor?"

"I don't think so. He sounds like he's on our side, yet it's hard to believe he's a party member. But he is certainly helping our cause."

"Couldn't we do something for him to show that we are grateful for everything that he has done for the Soviet Union?"

"I talked to the Chairman about it this morning. It's possible we might give him the Lenin Peace Prize next year."

"What about Chief of Police Bull Connor?"

"I think we could give him the Order of the Red Star."

"Good. It has always been my belief that when an American helps the Soviets in the cold war his efforts should be rewarded."

"I agree one hundred per cent. Without racial strife we'd have a very difficult time of it, and those people who make the racial strife are our friends whether they want to be or not."

"Perhaps we could show our appreciation to the police of Birmingham by sending them some dogs."

"The Chairman said we must be careful. If anyone suspects that we are interested in the race riots they might be stopped. We can't afford to have that."

"I agree, but it is difficult to sit and do nothing. The racists are doing so much for us and we can't do anything for them."

"We could make them honorary members of the Communist Party."

"That is an idea. I'll take it up with the Chairman tomorrow morning."

Making Extra Money

LAST TIME I WENT TO MIAMI BEACH I found the town in despair. A recent cold wave in Florida had received nationwide publicity, and the Miami Beach entrepreneurs couldn't seem to get their message over that Miami was once again a sunny playland and the frost had disappeared.

Hank Meyer, the official spokesman and drumbeater for Miami Beach, had done everything he could to get the message across, but with a newspaper strike in New York City, it was impossible to print photos of Florida beauties dipping their feet in the warm waters of the Atlantic, and without pictures who was going to believe it wasn't ski time at the Fontainebleau?

In desperation Mr. Meyer made out a rate card for newspapermen like myself.

"Every time you mention the word 'warm' in your column I'll pay you $1. I'll pay you $2 every time you mention the word 'hot' and $3 every time you mention the word 'sun.' If you mention Miami Beach in the same sentence, the price is double."

"But that's bribery," I said in a shocked voice. "How much will you give for the words 'beach,' 'swimming,' 'soft breeze,' and 'romance'?"

"Those are each worth 50 cents, used either as nouns or verbs."

"What about 'bathing beauties'?" I asked him.

"The 'bathing' part is worth 50 cents, but the 'beauties' are worth $3."

I realized I had discovered a way of making some extra Christmas money. "What about 'sun stroke'?" I asked excitedly.

"If you use 'sun stroke,'" Mr. Meyer said, "we have to penalize you $5. We don't want anyone to think it's THAT hot in Miami Beach."

"So 'boiling sun,' 'searing sands,' and 'burning rays' cannot be cashed in."

"They are definitely penalty words and will be taken out of your paycheck."

"What other words don't you want me to use?"

"'Cold,' 'frigid,' and 'icy' are all punishable by a $2 fine, except when used in referring to drinks such as 'icy Rum Collins.'"

"I don't assume you're paying anything for the word 'hurricane'?" I asked.

Mr. Meyer frowned. "The use of the word 'hurricane' in regard to Miami Beach will cost you $25."

"My, you're touchy," I said.

"And don't use 'chilly' either," he added. "That will cost you 50 cents."

Mr. Meyer said he wasn't trying to discourage us from making any money and there were exceptions for some words depending on their usage. "If you would like to make some extra money and use words like 'chilly,' 'frigid,' 'icy,' and 'cold,' we will pay $1 a word provided they are used in talking about the North, as in 'icy New York,' 'frigid Chicago,' and 'cold Connecticut.'"

Mr. Meyer then gave me a list of all the Miami Beach hotels and said the mention of any one of them in a newspaper article was worth $3.50.

"Even the Roney Plaza?" I said, because that's where I was staying.

Mr. Meyer pressed a button and Mr. David Schine, the owner of the Roney Plaza, came in and presented me with a check on the spot.

The Coast Watchers

DURING WORLD WAR II there was a group of men known as coast watchers, who were stationed on lonely islands in the Pacific to spy on enemy shipping and planes. These men performed a miraculous service for the Allied cause and everyone, including the President of the United States, owes them a debt of gratitude.

Since the potential enemy is now Cuba, the United States has set up coast watchers along the Florida coast, which is only ninety miles away from Cuba. The most concentrated of these are located at Miami Beach, where thousands of people have volunteered to spend their holidays sitting under beach umbrellas and staring out to sea, ready to sound the alarm in case of an invasion.

These selfless citizens, paying anywhere from thirty-five to sixty dollars a day for a place to sleep, have come from all over the United States by plane, train, and car to repulse the invader.

They're dug in at foxholes called the Fontainebleau, the Eden Roc, the Americana, and the Roney Plaza. They've taken up positions on the golf courses, the tennis courts, and the cabanas along this strategic beachhead. Subsisting on chopped chicken liver, steaks, roast beef, and lobster tails, the coast watchers of Miami Beach are ready for any kind of action.

As one of the first newspapermen permitted to visit Miami Beach since the Cuban crisis, I'm happy to report morale is high and most of the volunteers I talked to said they were not bitter about spending their holidays under a hot sun and a blue sky, if this is what their country asked of them.

One volunteer told me, "Sure, I'd rather be in Chicago in the snow, but somebody has to be here."

Another volunteer said, "I don't mind. After all, the President is down here, so who am I to complain about my assignment?"

"We knew what we were getting into when we volunteered," a woman in a bikini told me, "so we'll just go about our jobs without complaining."

I visited a command post at one of the hotels which have been taken over by civilians for coast watching.

"This is how we operate," an official told me. "Each volunteer spends four hours on the beach or by the swimming pool looking out toward Cuba. If he sees anything strange he shouts: 'Gin.' The unidentified object is then posted on the bulletin board. If it turns out to be friendly, the guest is charged an extra five dollars for towels. If the object proves to be a Cuban ship, the guest is given ten free dancing lessons in the Bongo-Bongo Room."

"You seem to be well-organized," I said.

"I should hope so," he said. "We don't have much time between the sighting of an unfriendly ship and the time we take action against one."

"What kind of action can you take?"

"Our strategy is to let the Cubans land unopposed and make them check in at one of the hotels along the beach. At the prices they're charging down here, Castro's men won't last more than three days. Then once they pay their hotel bills we'll throw them all in jail."

"And then what will you do with them?"

"We'll ransom them back to Cuba. What else?"

Separate But Equal Containers

MANY COMMUNITIES are concerned about the separation of church and state, but Los Angeles has a much more serious problem at the moment—and that is the separation of tin cans and garbage. When the city council passed a law that said Angelenos have to classify their refuse, and garbage was to be put out on one day and bottles and tin cans on another, everyone squawked from the Mayor on down to Jayne Mansfield. And when the council passed a law that anyone who didn't segregate his garbage would be liable to a five-hundred-dollar fine and six months in jail, the cries of anguish echoed from the hills of Hollywood to the streets of San Pedro.

I didn't realize how serious the issue was until I started talking to friends in Hollywood who were against separate but equal containers for garbage.

Allan Sherman, the folk singer, was disturbed by the logic of it all and told me, "Once you classify garbage, it's no longer garbage. The reason you call it garbage is that it is unclassified. Otherwise it becomes lettuce leaves, watermelon rinds, eggshells, clamshells, orange peels. We need filing cabinets instead of garbage pails to do the job properly."

Bill Dana, who plays José Jiminez on records and television, was even more disturbed. "I've never been good about separating garbage, even as a kid, and I was sure I would wind up in jail when the council passed the law. I could just see myself in a cell and a guy saying to me, 'What are you in for?' to which I'd have to reply, 'They found a broken Pepsi-Cola bottle in my rutabaga leaves.' Or, 'I was framed. My neighbor's kid tossed a Crackerjack box in with my TV dinner.'"

"How did the council plan on penalizing the people?" I asked.

"No one is quite sure because the council rescinded the law the next day," Mr. Sherman said, "but I have a friend in city hall and he said it would have worked something like this. If you threw an anchovy can into your garbage it would be considered a misdemeanor; a Campbell's tomato soup can would have meant a felony, and for a Dole's pineapple juice large-economy-size can they would have sent you to the gas chamber."

Mr. Dana told me the thing about garbage in Los Angeles is that it attracts flies and Los Angeles citizens have been urged to spray their garbage before putting it out.

"We have a saying in Los Angeles," he told me. "A family that sprays together stays together."

Mr. Sherman contributed this: one of the reasons people here have been less vociferous about the city council's doings in regard to garbage is that everyone is afraid to complain because the council might put into effect an alternate plan, known as Plan B.

The implementation of Plan B would mean that you could only dispose of garbage which began with the letter of the day. For example, on Monday the sanitation department would only collect things starting with "M," such as muskmelon, mint leaves, marcaroni, myrrh, and Melba toast. On Tuesday, you could only throw out tea bags, tomatoes, truffles, tripe, and tarts.

Mr. Dana said, "Plan B is unfair because only German-born people can throw out zwieback on Saturdays."

"What happens to the segregated garbage and tin cans?" I asked my friends.

"They take it to Arizona on freight trains," Mr. Sherman said, "and mix it all up together again."

I wanted to talk longer, but my friends had to go home and classify their garbage for the next day.

Mr. Dana was very philosophical about it. "Well, at least it keeps you from watching television."

10.

AD ASTRA PER
ASPIRIN

Confusion Is Rampant on Labeling Weapons

THERE IS a tremendous amount of confusion these days in determining what is an offensive weapon and what is a defensive weapon. The Cuban crisis forced everyone to make an agonizing reappraisal of weapons, and no one is quite sure now which is which.

Before Cuba it was quite simple to define the weapons. An offensive weapon was one that was pointed at you. A defensive weapon was one you pointed at the other guy. Everyone was quite sure the weapon pointed at you would be used against you, just as everyone was certain the one you pointed at the other guy would never be used except in the case of an attack. But it's very difficult now to use these definitions. Just the presence of a weapon on the enemy's soil could constitute an offensive weapon, even if it was pointed in the opposite direction. Weapons have become so sophisticated that if they are pointed in the opposite direction they can still be fired at you.

There is no problem in regard to small arms because, as members of "the Establishment," a satirical group now in New York, have pointed out, each bullet made today is marked with either a small "o" or a small "d." If someone fires a small "d" bullet at you, you know he is only doing it in defense, but if he fires a bullet with a small "o" on it, you know he is trying to kill you.

Unfortunately, the larger missiles and bombs are not so marked, and this is where the confusion begins. Only an expert can tell the difference between the offensive and defensive weapon, and even the experts can't agree among themselves.

Republican Senator Kenneth B. Keating of New York believes all weapons in Cuba are offensive ones. Therefore he is considered by Administration officials as an offensive Senator. Defense Secretary Robert S. McNamara, on the other hand, maintains that all weapons in Cuba are defensive ones, so he is considered by the Republicans as a very defensive Secretary of Defense.

When you get out of the realm of weapons, you still have offensive and defensive problems. Are the Russian troops stationed in Cuba offensive to us? We like to think so, and we've told Premier Khrushchev as much. But he refuses to take them out because he maintains they're technicians, and everyone knows technicians are only interested in defensive weapons.

Forgetting Cuba for a moment, when we offered Canada defensive weapons she took offense and the Government fell. When General Charles de Gaulle insisted on his own offensive weapons, we were so disappointed that in defense we gave the British Polaris missiles, which they accepted in place of the Skybolt, the only defensive weapon they had.

No one is satisfied with defensive weapons any more. Everyone wants the offensive kind. Offensive weapons are not only more accurate, but they can do more damage, particularly if they are fired first.

Senators like Barry Goldwater also feel you get your money's worth with an offensive weapon. A defensive weapon could sit on a launching pad for years and never be used. But an offensive weapon can be used any time. Besides that, offensive weapons are cheaper to make. You don't have to have such a long fuse.

The Truth About Skybolt

THERE HAS BEEN a lot of honest confusion about the Skybolt missile program and what it all means. Everyone knows that President Kennedy decided to cancel the Skybolt missile program and give Great Britain Polaris missiles instead. This caused a great deal of bitterness in the British Isles and anti-American fever went up several degrees.

For those who are not quite sure what happened, and I suppose Britain's Prime Minister Harold Macmillan could be included in this group, I'd like to explain the full story.

It seems that some time ago the British became very unhappy because they didn't have an independent nuclear deterrent. It has been the dream of every country in the Western Alliance, since the end of World War II, to have its own independent nuclear deterrent, so it can drop the bomb on someone if it feels like it without consulting the United States.

Having made the decision to have its own IND, the British sought out an independent nuclear deterrent company owned by two young men named Samuel Sky and Hugh Bolt. Sky and Bolt decided a missile was needed that could be shot from an airplane and hit its target a thousand miles away. They said such a missile could easily be perfected for $2,500,000,000.

"But we don't have two and a half billion dollars for such a project," the Chancellor of the Exchequer cried.

"Who does?" said the Minister of Defence.

"The Americans!" the rest of the Cabinet chorused.

"But how can we have an independent nuclear deterrent if the Americans put up the money for it?" the Minister for Housing said.

"Quite simple," said Sky.

"No sweat," said Bolt.

Then they explained their plan. It seems that the United States Air Force was also looking for an independent nuclear deterrent so they wouldn't be dependent on the United States Army or Navy in case of war. It was even more important to the United States Air Force to have an IND than it was to the British, for without one the Air Force would soon play a secondary role in the Pentagon, and would have as much to say in NATO as Luxembourg. Why not let the United States Air Force perfect the missile for the British? In exchange, the British would allow the Air Force to use it in case either the United States Navy or Army threatened the vital interests of Air Force Chief of Staff General Curtis E. LeMay.

Sky and Bolt were both knighted on the spot, not for the missile, but for saving the British $2,500,000,000.

The Air Force was delighted and went to work with fervor. Douglas Aircraft was hired to build the missile and pretty soon full-page color spreads appeared in all the magazines announcing the latest independent nuclear deterrent weapon.

Despite the advertising agency's enthusiasm the missile failed in five tests, and the Defense Department decided to cancel the program. This caused a great deal of consternation from California to the White Cliffs of Dover.

In England it was a question of pride. Without an independent nuclear deterrent of their own, the British would have to stop supporting President Moise Tshombe in Katanga.

But the United States Air Force was the bitterest of all. On the day after Mr. Macmillan was forced to give up his dream and accept the Polaris missile (developed by two Americans, Roger Pol and Arthur Laris) the Air Force decided to sink a Polaris submarine to prove they had the better weapon. Unfortunately the Skybolt went a hundred miles wide of its mark and the Defense Department told the Air Force to stop fooling around.

That more or less is what happened and explains why relations between Great Britain and the United States have become so strained. But while there is optimism that the breach between these two great nations will be healed, there

is a feeling here in Washington that the once friendly relations between the Air Force and the United States will never be the same.

Failures at the Cape Put DOF into Fast Orbit

THE CAPE CANAVERAL COMPLEX, made up of some of the most expensive hardware in the world, is one of the most exciting places in the world. Every day ten million to twenty million dollars' worth of missile is being shot up into the air in man's never-ending battle to find peaceful and warlike uses for space.

As far as I can tell, this is how Cape Canaveral works. The military develops a missile which when fired into space will blow up a country some five thousand miles away. Then the National Aeronautics and Space Administration, which is interested in peaceful uses of space, buys the missile from the military, and installs a capsule on the end of it to send a man into orbit.

At this point the military says, "You shouldn't send a man into space unless he has some military value. How about when he gets up there and we set up a space platform so we can shoot missiles at you-know-who?"

"Okay," says NASA. "You develop a space platform and we'll buy it from you to send our people to the moon."

"But the moon has no military value," the military protests. "It's hardly worth shooting at."

NASA then replies, "We're only interested in the peaceful uses of space."

"Sure," says the military, "you want us to solve all the problems of space so you can use it for exploration purposes. Don't you realize the Russians are trying to control space so they can control us?"

NASA says, "Look, you take care of the Russians, and we'll take care of the moon."

And so the conflict goes on. The Air Force, by virtue of its name, believes it should be in charge of space. The Army feels that when you get right down to it the foot soldier will eventually have to capture the planets, and therefore it should have a role in space. The Navy points out there are a lot of seas in outer space and since the Polaris submarine has already proved itself under water, Admiral Rickover should be in charge of the space program.

NASA, on the other hand, is getting the bulk of space funds and pretty soon it will be bigger than General Motors. NASA feels what's good for them is good for the country.

There have been many failures in our space race at Cape Canaveral, some on the ground, and some in the air. I can now report for the first time how they are handled. If a missile shot is a success, it is announced by the White House. If it's a failure, it's announced by Richard Nixon. And if the nose cone is recovered, Vice-President Lyndon Johnson is allowed to ride with it in a convertible up Broadway.

Nobody knows it but there is at Cape Canaveral a Department of Failures, known for short as DOF. The subcontract for this department was given to the Edsel Company, which has had more experience than anyone else in this type of work.

The DOF is located in a concrete bunker on the base and every man who works for it has been trained at a special school for masochists. As soon as a missile blows up on a pad or a satellite disappears in space, one of the DOF specialists comes out of his bunker and calls a press conference. He explains that although it is a random failure, it's only a temporary setback and steps are being taken to fix it.

"Don't get the idea this is going to slow down the program," he is permitted to say. "As a matter of fact, although the missile blew up on the pad, the scientific objective was accomplished and we learn more from our failures than we do from our successes. You have to roll with these things."

If the newspapermen persist in asking embarrassing questions, the spokesman is authorized to say, "When you get down to the nuts and bolts of this thing, we know for a fact that the Russians have had many more failures than we have had."

After the briefing the DOF man returns to his bunker where he sleeps on a bed made of needle-thin computer buttons.

There's a New Field for Hate Out Yonder

Is THERE ORGANIC LIFE in outer space? This is one of the major questions being asked in scientific circles today. Does this organic life resemble ours, and if not, what type of life exists on other planets? What effect will it have on us, first of all as Americans, and then secondly as human beings?

It is not too early to worry about these problems and to prepare for them. I have already started an organization to hate life in outer space. I feel, as do many of the people who have joined my society, that life in outer space presents a danger to every man, woman, and child in the world, and the public must be alerted to these dangers before we make the fateful step of being taken in by beings on other planets, who will in all probability try to dominate us.

There are some Munich-minded individuals who are prepared to make friends with the organisms in outer space. They are willing to trade our way of life for ways of life foreign to us. They are blind to the dangers of taking up with people—if you wish to call them that—who have none of the culture, the background, or the intelligence that we have on earth.

It is for this reason that the Society To Hate Life in Outer Space, or HALO, as it is known for short, was formed. We must combat all attempts to come to terms with life in outer space or lose our own in the attempt.

My society believes that there is something inhuman about life in outer space. If they were our friends, as they pretend to be, why haven't they made themselves known? Why haven't they come out and declared that there is life on other planets? What have they got to hide?

Obviously they're waiting for us to make the first move. They want us to go to them. They prefer to tackle our boys on their own territory. Surely they must know about our attempts to get into outer space, the money and time and effort that's being expended to reach them.

But have they co-operated in any way? Have they offered to pay part of the cost to get one of our people out to them? They have not. All attempts to reach them by radio and other communications have failed. They refuse to answer our calls, they ignore our wave lengths, they are probably laughing at us right now. It is typical of life in outer space to be sneaky, un-co-operative, and treacherous.

But once we make it to one of their planets, then what? Will we be greeted as scientists in search of new worlds to conquer? Will they understand that all we want to do is study them and find out what makes them tick? I hardly think so. First, they'll try to kill us. If their weapons are not up to ours, then they'll try to win us over and prey on our naïveté. If this doesn't succeed, they'll try to go to school with our children.

HALO is not waiting until men conquer space. We are preparing an educational program now which will prevent life in outer space from getting into our lives.

I think all books on outer space should be censored, and only those that affirm our way of life should be allowed on library bookshelves. I think all our astronauts should be briefed on the dangers of life in outer space. They should be able to recognize the enemy. Congress should hold hearings and call witnesses who have defected from outer space to show what could happen on our planet if outer-space organisms infiltrated our Government and labor unions.

We have the money for such a program. What we need now is the co-operation of every citizen. It isn't too early to join. Our slogan is: "Would you want someone from outer space to marry your sister?"

Button Plan Sews Up Prevention of A-War

ONE OF THE THINGS everyone has to worry about these days is the danger of an accidental war being set off with nuclear weapons. The best-selling book *Fail-Safe*, by Eugene Burdick and Harvey Wheeler, deals with this problem when a group of American bombers have gone past their fail-safe point, and because of some foul-up in a little black box, the bombers haven't gotten the word to come back. They are scheduled to blow up Moscow. To show the Russians it's all an accident, the President of the United States blows up New York, even though his wife is there on a shopping trip.

But there is another school in Washington that insists there are so many safeguards on atomic weapons that even if someone wanted to fire one he wouldn't be able to do it.

This is how this school sees it. In order to start a war, someone will have to push a button. To safeguard that no one will push the button accidentally, it is hidden every week in a different spot.

Only two people, both low-ranking military officers from different branches of the armed services, know the location of the button—but they don't know each other. Each has the authority to push the button when ordered to do so from higher up. But if both their thumbs are not on the button at the same time, it will not work.

Now let us suppose, by some stretch of the imagination, both men accidentally meet at the same location at the same time, and both decide to push the button at the same time. This does not automatically start World War III. When the button is pushed, all it does is turn on a green light in a bombproof, radiation-shielded, underground shelter in a secret place near Cheyenne, Wyoming. The shelter is manned by an enlisted Wac and an enlisted Wave, each of whom has a key to a white Princess telephone. As soon as they see the green light, they dial a secret number in South Dakota and say, "Condition Green."

This information is passed on to the quartermaster of the base, who immediately tries to contact Washington. But since he doesn't have the area code number for Washington, he can't dial directly. So he sends the message by carrier pigeon. This is known as "Condition Red."

As soon as the pigeon arrives in Washington, the Secretary of Defense is notified, and he in turn informs the President.

But the President cannot give the signal to do anything without turning a switch and there are seven locks on the switch. Each member of the Kennedy family has a key to one of the locks and the switch cannot be pulled unless all the locks are opened at the same time. Since the Kennedys are never in Washington all at the same time, it is virtually impossible for the President to pull the switch.

Therefore the chances of an accidental or even an intentional war are remote and shouldn't give anyone any sleepless nights. If it weren't for all these safeguards, I'd be worried too.

Fail-Peace

NOW THAT I HAVE dealt with the threat of accidental war and what it could mean to all of us, I would now like to deal with a subject that is even more frightening than accidental war. It is accidental peace.

Suppose someone got his signals mixed and by accident started a peace. You may say it's impossible, that it could never happen. But as men keep fooling around with things they don't know about, as our communications systems become more complex, as the pressures on the leaders who hold the key to our future become greater, there is always the chance that someone might set off a peace that no one could control.

In a new book that I'm writing called "Fail-Peace," I have presented just such a situation. I tell how, with all the safeguards both sides have at their command, someone triggers off the greatest peace that man has ever known.

My story opens in Geneva during one of the many disarmament conferences. A lowly clerk in the American delegation pushes the wrong button on his decoding machine, and discovers that the Russians have launched what could possibly be a peace offer. He reports it to his superiors, who immediately call Washington.

"We can't be sure," the ambassador tells the President, "but we think the Russians are about to declare peace."

"It could be a false alarm," the President says. "We've had these alerts before."

"Yes, sir, but I think we should be prepared in case it's the real thing."

"All right, I'll put Operation Good Will to Men into effect."

The President pushes a button that sounds an alarm in bases all over the country. "Now hear this, now hear this," commanders announce to their men, "a Russian peace proposal has been spotted over Geneva. This may be a test or it could mean the real thing. If it's the real thing, be prepared to cancel all defense contracts and destroy all stockpiles in this country."

In the meantime, the Russians have received word that the Americans have put their armed forces on a peace alert and they get ready to meet the attack. Five Russian divisions are demobilized, an atomic testing station in the Urals is destroyed, and forty new Soviet submarines are flooded and sunk.

The Americans pick up this information and they immediately sink fourteen of their own missile cruisers, slash the tires on every SAC bomber, and order all Polaris warheads to be destroyed at sea.

The Russians immediately react and start breaking up their ICBM missile sites, demobilize another two hundred divisions, and kick all army officers out of the Presidium.

The President closes down the Pentagon, furloughs the Joint Chiefs of Staff, and fires the United States Marine Corps Band.

Both sides are eyeball to eyeball, headed hell-bent toward a peaceful showdown, and nobody blinks.

At the last minute the error is discovered. The Russian peace proposal in Geneva, it turns out, is not the real thing.

The President is aghast. Is it too late to stop the destruction of the United States military machine? How will the Russian Premier act when he realizes the disarmament he has been forced into was all a mistake?

The President decides there is only one thing to do. He telephones Moscow and tells the Soviet leader there has been an accident and chances of peace are imminent. He asks the Russian if there is anything he can do to avert an all-out *détente*.

The Soviet leader is sympathetic. "It's nobody's fault," he says. "We'll start from scratch again. Neither one of us can afford an all-out peace at this time."

Relieved, everyone goes back to doing things the way they were done before. New safeguards are put on the decoding machines to prevent such an accident from ever happening again.

This book was set in

Caledonia and Perpetua types by

Harry Sweetman Typesetting Corporation.

It was printed and bound at the press of

The World Publishing Company.

Design is by Larry Kamp.